GRANDMA'S BEST RECIPES

GRANDMA'S BEST RECIPES

Love Food™ is an imprint of Parragon Books Ltd

Parragon
Queen Street House
4 Queen Street
Bath BA1 1HE, UK

Copyright © Parragon Books Ltd 2007

Love Food™ and the accompanying heart device is a trademark of Parragon Books Ltd

ISBN 978-1-4054-9484-7

Internal design by Jane Bozzard-Hill
Cover design by Mark Cavanagh
Photography by Bob Wheeler
Home economists: Sandra Baddeley and Valerie Barrett
Introduction by Pamela Gwyther

Printed in China

Notes for the reader
This book uses imperial, metric, and U.S. cup measurements. Follow the same units of
measurement throughout; do not mix imperial and metric. All spoon measurements are
level, unless otherwise stated; teaspoons are assumed to be 5 ml, and tablespoons are
assumed to be 15 ml. Unless otherwise stated, milk is assumed to be whole, eggs and
individual fruits, such as bananas, are medium, and pepper is freshly ground black pepper.

Recipes using raw or lightly cooked eggs should be avoided by infants, the elderly,
pregnant women, convalescents, and anyone suffering from an illness. Pregnant and
breast-feeding women are advised to avoid eating peanuts and peanut products.

$\mathcal{C}$ONTENTS

$\mathcal{I}$NTRODUCTION

This book is all about our favorite childhood food memories, and it will give you the opportunity to create dishes "just like Grandma used to make." It will conjure up the wonderful food smells that would always be present when we went to visit our grandparents as children, and the warm home-cooked meals that were waiting for us. It would be particularly welcoming to arrive when Grandma had just been baking and there was a selection of cakes and cookies, and even freshly baked bread to smother with butter and eat fresh from the oven. Grandma's food was always a comfort; just the thing to cheer you up, soothe a cold, or even help heal a broken heart. Like Grandma herself, her food was always there and could be relied upon in all circumstances.

"Grandma's food was always a comfort—just the thing to cheer you up"

For many of us, our childhoods were very much linked to our grandparents. When we visited them for Christmas and other holidays, all the traditional foods would appear as if by magic. It is only with hindsight that we appreciate the amount of planning and hard work that went into making our perfect holidays. Often we would not only be able to eat the food but have the thrill of helping to make it. Somehow Grandma always had time to allow us to roll out the pie dough and cookies and help mix the cakes. She even allowed us to lick the wooden spoon and scrape the mixing bowl to try the delicious batter before it went into the oven. It was here that many of us learned to cook, as Grandma was able to spend time with us and pass on the considerable knowledge that she had acquired over the years.

Weekends spent at our grandparents often meant a traditional meal would be served. In addition to a huge roast, there would be all the accompaniments: the vegetables, mashed potatoes, carrots, oodles of gravy, and always dinner rolls hot from the oven. The meal would be followed by a wonderful dessert—apple pie, peach cobbler, or maybe a Key lime pie. When there was a celebration, like a birthday, there might even be a Black Forest cake or an ice cream cake with candles for the birthday girl or boy to blow out.

The food Grandma prepared for everyday meals was simpler. First, because times were tough in her day, she would make the best use of leftovers to come up with dishes such as beef pot pie and potato dumplings using the remnants from the Sunday meal. Meals tended to be fairly heavy, as people often had to do more physical work and didn't have cars, so they would walk relatively long distances. Casseroles and stews using the cheaper cuts of meat were prepared and cooked for a long time in a slow oven so that the meat would be tender. Sausages and potatoes were also popular, as they were filling and economical. Vegetables were often home grown, so they would be fresh and in season. Some of the surplus vegetables and fruits would be preserved for use later in the year—fruit was turned into jam and vegetables were salted or pickled.

Today's generation of grandmothers is likely to be engaged full time in the workplace and trying to juggle home, family, work, hobbies, interests, and travels abroad. Her time for cooking has been reduced and she probably saves the traditional foods for special occasions and chooses quicker and healthier recipes in her day-to-day cooking. Her food habits are changing, too, influenced by travel to far-away places and sampling the local fare. Today's multicultural society also means that we

*"Like Grandma herself, her food could be relied upon
in all circumstances"*

eat different foods on different occasions and celebrate new festivals. We also have a wider variety of food ingredients available, making many new recipes and meals far more accessible.

As the years have passed, our eating habits have changed. Foods that would have been considered exotic twenty years ago have become part of our everyday life—and comfort foods in their own right. Although pizza has long been a national favorite, dishes such as chicken Kiev, spaghetti bolognese, and chili con carne have also been absorbed into our national identity. This is a result of the changing population of our own country and the fact that many of us now have the opportunity to travel throughout the world. Most of our grandparents did not get the chance to journey much farther than their own backyards, but global travel has widened the range of food experiences for today's generation. South American, Asian, and Eastern European foods have all become part of our regular diet in recent years.

The way we eat has also changed over recent years. Although many will say it's a shame that families don't regularly sit down together for meals anymore, some food habits have changed

for the better. We eat a lighter diet and consume more good quality fresh fruits and vegetables that are available throughout the year. We are much more aware of what foods are good for us, although our busy lifestyles often lead us to make unwise food choices and give in to the convenience of packaged foods and take-out.

But on the weekend, when we have more time, our favorite recipes come into their own. Although they may have a newer twist or include a prepared ingredient like a frozen pie crust, essentially they are the foods we ate in our childhood. And when there is a birthday or anniversary, we tend to make more of an effort in preparing the food and are more extravagant with its selection. This is also the time when we might bake, providing family or friends with a special treat, like gingerbread or coffee cake, to accompany a cup of coffee. Some people spend some of their time on the weekend preparing home-cooked food and then freezing it for later in the week. In order to do this you need to be organized and have large saucepans available so that you can cook in large quantities, but it is often worth the effort.

Comfort foods are the old favorites: the meals that are particularly familiar to us, make us feel warm inside, and soothe our souls. Grandma made these for us when we were young, so the good feelings associated with them are still there. When we are upset, worried, or depressed, simple food like a warming chicken or tomato soup is just what we need. Dishes that you can eat with your hands, such as a grilled cheese sandwich or a tasty hamburger, are just the thing when you don't feel like sitting at the table with a

GRANDMA'S COMFORT FOOD

knife and fork. A casserole is an excellent standby for a cold winter's day and provides a great opportunity to get the family to sit around the table, to eat and talk about the day. Other familiar foods, like traditional roast chicken, fish pie, and baked potatoes, are all covered in this chapter so whenever you need them, you'll have heartening recipes on hand, just like the ones your Grandma might have cooked for you.

TOMATO SOUP

SERVES 4
4 tbsp butter
I onion, finely chopped
I lb 9 oz/700 g tomatoes, finely chopped
salt and pepper
2½ cups hot chicken or vegetable stock

pinch of sugar
2 tbsp shredded fresh basil leaves, plus
   extra sprigs for garnish
I tbsp chopped fresh parsley
croutons, for serving (optional)

GRANDMA'S TIPS

*When fresh tomatoes are out
of season and tasteless, use
1 lb 12 oz/800 g canned
tomatoes. Not only will they give
some extra sweetness to your
soup, using canned tomatoes will
save you some time. For a special
treat and for extra warmth in
the winter, add a tablespoon
of sherry to each bowl before
serving.*

1 Melt half the butter in a large, heavy-bottom pan. Add the onion and cook over low heat, stirring occasionally, for 5 minutes, or until softened. Add the tomatoes, season to taste with salt and pepper, and cook for 5 minutes.

2 Pour in the hot stock, return to a boil, then reduce the heat, and cook for 10 minutes.

3 Push the soup through a strainer with the back of a wooden spoon to remove the tomato skins and seeds. Return to the pan and stir in the sugar, remaining butter, basil, and parsley. Heat through briefly, but do not let boil. Ladle into warmed serving bowls. Serve immediately, garnished with sprigs of basil and accompanied by croutons, if you wish.

CHICKEN SOUP

SERVES 4
3 tbsp butter
4 shallots, chopped
1 leek, trimmed and sliced
1 lb/450 g skinless chicken breasts, chopped
2½ cups chicken stock

1 tbsp chopped fresh parsley
1 tbsp chopped fresh thyme
salt and pepper
¾ cup heavy cream
sprigs of fresh thyme, for garnish
fresh crusty rolls, for serving

GRANDMA'S TIPS

If you have just cooked a whole chicken for a meal, you can make a stock with the leftovers. Place the carcass in a large saucepan of water along with a chopped onion, carrot, and celery stalk. Bring to a boil, then simmer for 1–1¼ hours. Strain and carefully remove any meat from the bones and set aside. Make the soup according to the recipe, adding the cooked chicken pieces either before blending or just before serving.

1 Melt the butter in a large pan over medium heat. Add the shallots and cook, stirring, for 3 minutes, until slightly softened. Add the leek and cook for another 5 minutes, stirring. Add the chicken, stock, and herbs, and season with salt and pepper. Bring to a boil, then lower the heat and simmer for 25 minutes, until the chicken is tender and cooked through. Remove from the heat and let cool for 10 minutes.

2 Transfer the soup into a food processor and blend until smooth (you may need to do this in batches). Return the soup to the pan and warm over low heat for 5 minutes.

3 Stir in the cream and cook for another 2 minutes, then remove from the heat and ladle into serving bowls. Garnish with sprigs of thyme and serve with fresh crusty rolls.

GRILLED CHEESE SANDWICH

SERVES 2
3½ oz/100 g Gruyère or Emmental
   cheese, grated
4 slices white bread, with the crusts
   trimmed
2 thick slices ham
1 small egg, beaten
3 tbsp unsalted butter, plus extra if
   necessary

for the white sauce
2 tbsp unsalted butter
1 tsp corn oil
½ tbsp all-purpose flour
½ cup warm milk
pepper

1 Spread half the cheese on 2 bread slices, then top each with a slice of ham, cut to fit. Sprinkle the ham with all but 2 tablespoons of the remaining cheese, then sandwich together with the remaining bread slices and press down well.

2 To make the sauce, melt the butter with the oil in a small, heavy-bottom pan and stir in the flour until well combined and smooth. Cook over medium heat, stirring constantly, for 1 minute. Remove from the heat and stir in a little of the milk until well incorporated. Return to the heat and gradually add the remaining milk, stirring constantly, until it has all been incorporated. Cook for an additional 3 minutes, or until the sauce is smooth and thickened. Stir in the remaining cheese and pepper to taste, then set aside and keep warm.

3 Beat the egg in a shallow dish. Add 1 sandwich and press down to coat on both sides, then remove from the dish and repeat with the other sandwich.

4 Preheat the broiler to high. Line a cookie sheet with foil and set aside. Melt the butter in a sauté pan or skillet and cook 1 or both sandwiches, depending on the size of your pan, over medium-high heat until golden brown on both sides. Add a little extra butter, if necessary, if you have to cook the sandwiches separately.

5 Transfer the sandwiches to the foil-lined cookie sheet and spread the white sauce over the top. Cook under the broiler, about 4 inches/10 cm from the heat, for 4 minutes, or until golden and brown.

SLOPPY JOES

SERVES 4
1 tbsp sunflower or corn oil
1 onion, finely chopped
1 red bell pepper, cored, seeded, and finely chopped
1 lb/450 g ground beef
1 tbsp all-purpose flour
½ tsp dried thyme

1 ¼ cups canned condensed cream of tomato soup
½ cup water
½ tbsp Worcestershire sauce, or to taste
salt and pepper
4 sesame seed buns
French fries, for serving

GRANDMA'S TIPS

The cooked meat mixture can be served without the bun—pour over baked potatoes or on top of a bowl of pasta for a tasty supper dish. Kids will love the sweet, soft texture.

1 Heat the oil in a large skillet or pan over medium-high heat. Add the onion and bell pepper and cook, stirring frequently, for 5–8 minutes until soft but not browned. Add the beef and cook, stirring constantly and breaking up the meat with a wooden spoon, until no pinkness remains.

2 Sprinkle in the flour and thyme and cook, stirring constantly, for an additional 2 minutes.

3 Stir in the soup, water, Worcestershire sauce, and salt and pepper to taste. Bring to a boil, then reduce the heat and simmer, stirring occasionally, for 15 minutes, or until the mixture thickens and the beef is cooked through.

4 Put the bottom half of each bun on an individual serving plate. Spoon over the Sloppy Joe mixture and replace the top halves. Serve with French fries on the side.

ROAST CHICKEN

SERVES 6
1 free-range chicken, weighing 5 lb/
   2.25 kg
4 tbsp butter
2 tbsp chopped fresh lemon thyme

salt and pepper
1 lemon, quartered
½ cup white wine
6 fresh thyme sprigs, for garnish

GRANDMA'S TIPS

This is the quintessential simple roast chicken recipe. But if you want to add even more flavor to the bird, stuff it with a finely chopped onion, the grated rind and juice of 1 lemon, and some fresh thyme leaves mixed with a few soft breadcrumbs. For an even more robust variation, stuff the bird with 40 cloves of garlic—it will be delicious and milder than you might think, as the cooking renders the garlic sweet and not so pungent.

1 Preheat the oven to 425°F/220°C. Make sure the chicken is clean, wiping it inside and out using paper towels, and place in a roasting pan.

2 Place the butter in a bowl and soften with a fork, then mix in the thyme and season well with salt and pepper. Butter the chicken all over with the herb butter, inside and out, and place the lemon quarters inside the body cavity. Pour the wine over the chicken.

3 Roast the chicken in the center of the oven for 20 minutes. Reduce the temperature to 375°F/190°C and continue to roast for an additional 1¼ hours, basting frequently. Cover with foil if the skin starts to brown too much. If the pan dries out, add a little more wine or water.

4 Test that the chicken is cooked by piercing the thickest part of the leg with a sharp knife or skewer and making sure the juices run clear. Remove from the oven.

5 Remove the chicken from the roasting pan and place on a warmed serving plate to rest, covered with foil, for 10 minutes before carving.

6 Place the roasting pan on the top of the stove and bubble the pan juices gently over low heat until they have reduced and are thick and glossy. Season to taste with salt and pepper.

7 Serve the chicken with the pan juices and sprinkle with the thyme sprigs.

SOUTHERN FRIED CHICKEN

SERVES 4–6
1 chicken, weighing 3 lb 5 oz/1.5 kg,
  cut into 6 or 8 pieces
salt and pepper

½ cup all-purpose flour
2–4 tbsp butter
corn or peanut oil, for pan-frying
mashed potatoes, for serving

1 Put the chicken into a large bowl with 1 teaspoon of salt and cold water to cover, then cover the bowl and let stand in the refrigerator for at least 4 hours, but ideally overnight. Drain the chicken pieces well and pat completely dry with paper towels.

2 Put the flour and salt and pepper to taste into a plastic bag, hold closed, and shake to mix. Add the chicken pieces and shake until well coated. Remove the chicken pieces from the bag and shake off any excess flour.

3 Melt 2 tablespoons of the butter with about ½ inch/1 cm of oil in an ovenproof casserole or large skillet with a lid over medium-high heat.

4 Add as many chicken pieces as will fit in a single layer without overcrowding, skin-side down. Cook for 5 minutes, or until the skin is golden and crisp. Turn the chicken over and cook for an additional 10–15 minutes, covered, until it is tender and the juices run clear when a skewer is inserted into the thickest part of the meat. Remove the chicken from the casserole with a slotted spoon and drain well on paper towels. Transfer to a low oven to keep warm while cooking any remaining pieces, if necessary, or let cool completely. Remove any brown bits from the dish and melt the remaining butter in the oil, adding more oil as needed, to cook the next batch. Serve hot or cold with mashed potatoes.

POT ROAST

SERVES 6
2½ tbsp all-purpose flour
1 tsp salt
¼ tsp pepper
1 rolled brisket joint, weighing 3 lb 8 oz/
    1.6 kg
2 tbsp vegetable oil
2 tbsp butter
1 onion, finely chopped

2 celery stalks, diced
2 carrots, peeled and diced
1 tsp dill seed
1 tsp dried thyme or oregano
1½ cups red wine
⅔–1 cup beef stock
4–5 potatoes, cut into large chunks and
    boiled until just tender
2 tbsp chopped fresh dill, for serving

GRANDMA'S TIPS

This is the best way to tenderize tougher cuts of meat. You can also cook the pot roast in a slow cooker on the low setting to make the meat extra soft and tender.

1 Preheat the oven to 275°F/140°C.

2 Mix 2 tablespoons of the flour with the salt and pepper in a shallow dish. Dip the meat to coat. Heat the oil in an ovenproof casserole and brown the meat all over. Transfer to a plate.

3 Add half the butter to the casserole and cook the onion, celery, carrots, dill seed, and thyme for 5 minutes. Return the meat and juices to the casserole.

4 Pour in the wine and enough stock to reach one-third of the way up the meat. Bring to a boil, cover, and cook in the oven for 3 hours, turning the meat every 30 minutes. After it has been cooking for 2 hours, add the potatoes and more stock if necessary.

5 When ready, transfer the meat and vegetables to a warmed serving dish. Strain the cooking liquid into a pan.

6 Mix the remaining butter and flour to a paste. Bring the cooking liquid to a boil. Whisk in small pieces of the flour and butter paste, whisking constantly until the sauce is smooth. Pour the sauce over the meat and vegetables. Sprinkle with the fresh dill to serve.

BEEF STEW WITH DUMPLINGS

SERVES 6
3 tbsp olive oil
2 onions, finely sliced
2 garlic cloves, chopped
2 lb 4 oz/1 kg good-quality braising beef
2 tbsp all-purpose flour
salt and pepper
1 cup beef stock
bouquet garni
½ cup red wine
1 tbsp chopped fresh parsley, for garnish

for the herb dumplings
scant 1 cup self-rising flour, plus extra
  for shaping
4 tbsp suet or vegetable shortening
1 tsp mustard
1 tbsp chopped fresh parsley
1 tsp chopped fresh sage
salt and pepper
4 tbsp cold water

GRANDMA'S TIPS
You can make the stew the day before and refrigerate it overnight. Reheat for 20 minutes before adding the dumplings, and proceed with the recipe. Precooking will enhance the flavor of the stew and makes for fresh and light dumplings. You can vary the herbs used—try rosemary or thyme—and add some crushed garlic if you like.

1 Preheat the oven to 300°F/150°C.

2 Heat 1 tablespoon of the oil in a large skillet and sauté the onion and garlic until softened and lightly browned. Remove from the pan using a slotted spoon and place in a large casserole dish.

3 Trim the meat and cut it into thick strips. Using the remaining oil, sauté the meat in the skillet over high heat, stirring well until it is browned all over.

4 Sprinkle in the flour and stir well to avoid lumps from forming. Season well with salt and pepper.

5 Reduce the heat to medium, pour in the stock, stirring constantly to make a smooth sauce, then continue to heat until boiling.

6 Carefully turn the contents of the skillet into the casserole dish. Add the bouquet garni and wine. Cover, place in the oven, and bake for 2–2½ hours.

7 Start making the dumplings 20 minutes before the stew is ready. Place the flour, suet, mustard, parsley, sage, and salt and pepper to taste in a bowl and mix well. Just before adding the dumplings to the stew, add enough of the water to the mixture to form a firm but soft dough. Break the dough into 12 pieces and roll them into round dumplings (you might need to flour your hands for this).

8 Remove the stew from the oven, check the seasoning, discard the bouquet garni, and add the dumplings, pushing them down under the liquid. Cover and return the dish to the oven, and continue to cook for 15 minutes or until the dumplings have doubled in size.

9 Serve piping hot with the parsley scattered over the top.

STEAK & FRENCH FRIES

SERVES 4

for the Maître d'Hôtel butter
½ cup butter
3 tbsp finely chopped fresh parsley
1 tbsp lemon juice
salt and pepper

for the French fries
1 lb 8 oz/675 g large potatoes
sunflower, corn, or peanut oil,
   for deep-frying

for the steaks
4 sirloin, porterhouse, or tenderloin
   steaks, about 6–8 oz/175–225 g each
olive or sunflower oil, for brushing and
   oiling
pepper

salad greens, for serving

1 First, make the Maître d'Hôtel butter. Put the butter into a bowl and beat with a wooden spoon until softened. Add the parsley and lemon juice, season to taste with salt and pepper, and blend together until well mixed. Turn the mixture out onto a sheet of waxed paper and shape into a roll. Wrap in the waxed paper and let chill in the refrigerator for 2–3 hours until firm. The butter can be made well in advance and stored in the refrigerator for up to 4–5 days or can be wrapped in foil and stored in the freezer until needed.

2 Peel the potatoes and cut into ½-inch/1-cm even-size fry shapes. As soon as they are prepared, put them into a large bowl of cold water to prevent discoloration, then let soak for 30 minutes to remove the excess starch. Drain the potatoes and dry well on a clean dish towel. Heat the oil in a deep-fryer or large, heavy-bottom pan to 375°F/190°C. If you do not have a thermometer, test the temperature by dropping a piece of potato into the oil. If it sinks, the oil isn't hot enough; if it floats and the oil bubbles around it, it is ready. Add the potatoes to the oil in small batches and deep-fry for 5–6 minutes until soft but not browned. Remove from the oil and drain well on paper towels. Remember to let the oil return to the correct temperature between each batch.

3 Preheat the broiler. Brush each steak with oil and season to taste with pepper. Put each steak onto an oiled broiler rack and cook under medium heat for the required length of time and according to your taste: for ¾-inch/2-cm thick steaks, 5 minutes for rare, 8–10 minutes for medium, and 12–14 minutes for well done; for 1-inch/2.5-cm thick steaks, 6–7 minutes for rare, 8–10 minutes for medium, and 12–15 minutes for well done; for 1½-inch/4-cm thick steaks, 10 minutes for rare, 12–14 minutes for medium, and 18–20 minutes for well done. During cooking, turn the steaks frequently using a spatula and brush them once or twice with oil.

4 While the steaks are cooking, reheat the oil in the deep-fryer to 400°F/200°C. Add the potatoes, in small batches, and deep-fry for 2–3 minutes until golden brown. Remove from the oil and drain on paper towels.

5 Serve each broiled steak at once, topped with a slice of Maître d'Hôtel butter and accompanied by French fries and salad greens.

HAMBURGERS

SERVES 4–6
1 lb/450 g rump steak or top round,
   freshly ground
1 onion, grated
2–4 garlic cloves, crushed
2 tsp whole-grain mustard
pepper
2 tbsp olive oil

1 lb/450 g onions, finely sliced
2 tsp brown sugar

for serving
4–6 sesame seed buns
salad greens
ketchup (optional)

GRANDMA'S TIPS

It's always handy to have hamburgers prepared and at the ready so that you can cook them quickly when needed. Make a large batch and freeze them on a baking sheet, then wrap them individually or store them in a plastic container with parchment between the burgers to separate them. Prepare the hamburgers directly from the freezer, but make sure they are cooked through before serving.

1 Place the ground steak, grated onion, garlic, mustard, and pepper to taste in a large bowl and mix together. Shape into 4–6 equal-size burgers, then cover and let chill for 30 minutes.

2 Meanwhile, heat the oil in a heavy-bottom skillet. Add the onions and cook over low heat for 10–15 minutes, or until the onions have caramelized. Add the sugar after 8 minutes and stir occasionally during cooking. Drain well on paper towels and keep warm.

3 Wipe the skillet clean, then heat until hot. When hot, add the burgers and cook for 3–5 minutes on each side or until cooked to personal preference. Serve in sesame seed buns with the onions, salad greens, and ketchup, if you like.

MEATLOAF

SERVES 6
1 thick slice crustless white bread
3 cups freshly ground beef, pork, or lamb
1 small egg
1 tbsp finely chopped onion
1 beef bouillon cube, crumbled
1 tsp dried mixed herbs
salt and pepper

for serving
tomato or mushroom sauce or gravy
mashed potatoes
freshly cooked green beans

GRANDMA'S TIPS

To make a traditional-shaped loaf, use a small loaf pan. Grease the pan well or line with foil. Spoon the mixture into the pan, smooth the surface, and cook according to the recipe. You can also line the pan with bacon strips or slices of pancetta to keep the meat moist and add extra flavor to the meatloaf.

1 Preheat the oven to 350°F/180°C.

2 Put the bread into a small bowl and add enough water to soak. Let stand for 5 minutes, then drain and squeeze well to get rid of all the water.

3 Combine the bread and all the other ingredients in a bowl. Shape into a loaf, then place on a cookie sheet or in an ovenproof dish. Put the meatloaf in the oven and cook for 30–45 minutes until the juices run clear when it is pierced with a toothpick.

4 Serve in slices with your favorite sauce or gravy, mashed potatoes, and green beans.

LAMB SHANKS

SERVES 4

9 oz/250 g cannellini beans, soaked
   overnight
2 tbsp sunflower or corn oil
1 large onion, thinly sliced
4 carrots, chopped
2 celery stalks, thinly sliced
1 garlic clove, chopped
4 large lamb shanks

14 oz/400 g canned chopped tomatoes
1¼ cups red wine
finely pared zest and juice of 1 orange
2 bay leaves
3 rosemary sprigs
scant 1 cup water
salt and pepper

1 Preheat the oven to 325°F/160°C. Drain the soaked beans and rinse under cold
running water. Put in a large pan of cold water, bring to a boil, and skim off any foam,
then boil rapidly for 10 minutes. Drain and set aside.

2 Meanwhile, heat the oil in a large, flameproof casserole, add the onion, and cook
for 5 minutes, or until softened. Add the carrots and celery and cook for an additional
5 minutes, or until beginning to soften and the onion is beginning to brown. Add the
garlic and cook for an additional 1 minute. Push the vegetables to the sides of the pan.

3 Add the lamb shanks to the pan and cook for about 5 minutes, until browned on all
sides. Add the beans to the pan with the tomatoes, wine, and orange zest and juice and
stir together. Add the bay leaves and rosemary. Pour in the water so that the liquid comes
halfway up the shanks. Season with pepper but do not add salt as this will stop the beans
from softening.

4 Bring to a boil, then cover the pan and cook in the oven for about 1 hour. Turn the
shanks over in the stock then continue cooking for 1½ hours until the lamb and beans
are tender. Remove the bay leaves, then taste and add salt and pepper if necessary.
Serve hot.

SAUSAGES & ONIONS

SERVES 4
8 fresh bratwurst sausages, pricked all
   over with a fork
about 2 tbsp sunflower or corn oil
   (as needed)
2 onions, thinly sliced
2 garlic cloves, sliced

2 cups pilsner lager
1 tbsp German brown mustard or
   coarse-grain mustard, plus extra
   for serving
salt and pepper
chunks of Italian or French bread,
   for serving

1 Heat a large skillet or flameproof casserole with a tight-fitting lid over medium-high heat. Add as many sausages as will fit in a single layer and cook, stirring frequently, until browned all over. Remove from the skillet and set aside. Brown the remaining sausages, if necessary.

2 Add extra oil to the sausage fat in the skillet, if necessary, to make about 2 tablespoons in total. Add the onions to the pan and cook, stirring frequently, for 5 minutes. Add the garlic and cook, stirring frequently, for an additional 5 minutes, or until the onions are soft and lightly browned.

3 Stir in the lager, scraping the base of the skillet with a wooden spoon. Return the sausages to the skillet. Increase the heat to high and bring the lager to a boil, then reduce the heat to low, cover tightly, and simmer for 20 minutes.

4 Stir in the mustard and simmer, uncovered, for a few minutes until most of the lager has evaporated. Season to taste with salt and pepper.

5 Serve the sausages split lengthwise down the center with the onions spooned over. Serve with chunks of bread and a small jar of mustard on the side.

TUNA-NOODLE CASSEROLE

SERVES 4–6

7 oz/200 g dried egg ribbon pasta, such as tagliatelle
2 tbsp butter
2 oz/55 g fine fresh breadcrumbs
1¾ cups canned condensed cream of mushroom soup
4 fl oz/125 ml milk
2 celery stalks, chopped

1 red and 1 green bell pepper, cored, seeded, and chopped
5 oz/140 g sharp Cheddar cheese, coarsely grated
2 tbsp chopped fresh parsley
7 oz/200 g canned tuna in oil, drained and flaked
salt and pepper

GRANDMA'S TIPS

You can use other varieties of pasta for this dish; macaroni or fusilli work well, and kids will like alphabet or animal pasta shapes. The tuna can be replaced with canned salmon or crab or even pieces of cooked chicken—whatever your family likes best.

1 Preheat the oven to 400°F/200°C. Bring a large pan of water to a boil. Add the pasta and cook for 2 minutes less than specified on the package instructions.

2 Meanwhile, melt the butter in a separate, small pan over medium heat. Stir in the breadcrumbs, then remove from the heat and set aside.

3 Drain the pasta well and set aside. Pour the soup into the pasta pan over medium heat, then stir in the milk, celery, bell peppers, half the cheese, and the parsley. Add the tuna and gently stir in so that the flakes don't break up. Season to taste with salt and pepper. Heat just until small bubbles appear around the edges of the mixture—do not boil.

4 Stir the pasta into the pan and use 2 forks to mix all the ingredients together. Spoon the mixture into an ovenproof dish that is also suitable for serving, and spread out.

5 Stir the remaining cheese into the buttered breadcrumbs, then sprinkle over the top of the pasta mixture. Bake in the oven for 20–25 minutes until the topping is golden. Let stand for 5 minutes before serving straight from the dish.

FISH PIE

SERVES 6

2 tbsp butter, plus extra for greasing
2 onions, chopped
2 lb 4 oz/1 kg cod fillet, skinned and
  cut into strips
4 rindless lean bacon strips, cut into
  ½-inch/1-cm wide slices
2 tbsp chopped fresh parsley

salt and pepper
14 oz/400 g canned great Northern
  beans, drained and rinsed
2½ cups milk
1 lb 2 oz/500 g potatoes, very thinly
  sliced

1 Preheat the oven to 350°F/180°C. Lightly grease a flameproof casserole with a little butter. Arrange the onions in the bottom and cover with the strips of fish and bacon. Sprinkle with the parsley and season to taste with salt and pepper.

2 Add the great Northern beans, then pour in the milk. Arrange the potato slices over the top, overlapping them slightly, to cover the entire surface of the pie.

3 Dot the potato slices with the butter. Bake the pie in the oven for 40 minutes, or until the potatoes are crisp and golden. Serve immediately.

SALMON FISHCAKES

SERVES 4

1 lb 9 oz/700 g skinless salmon fillet, cut into cubes
1 ¼ cups whole milk
1 bay leaf
3 ½ oz/100 g broccoli, steamed until tender
1 lb 9 oz/700 g potatoes, boiled and mashed
2 tbsp minced fresh parsley
4 tbsp whole wheat flour
pepper
1 egg yolk
2 large eggs, beaten
2 ¾ cups fresh whole wheat breadcrumbs
2 tbsp olive oil

GRANDMA'S TIPS

These absolutely delicious luxury fishcakes can be made more economical by using canned salmon. The broccoli can be replaced with sautéed leeks or even corn kernels, which the kids will love. For a more sophisticated flavor, chopped dill can be used instead of the parsley, and the fishcakes can be served with a dill sauce or mayonnaise.

1 Preheat the oven to 400°F/200°C. Put the salmon in a pan with the milk and bay leaf and bring slowly up to a simmer. Let simmer for 2 minutes, then remove the pan from the heat, lift out and discard the bay leaf, and leave the fish in the milk to cool. When cooled, lift out the fish with a slotted spoon onto paper towels to drain.

2 Flake the fish into a large bowl. Put the broccoli in a food processor and pulse until smooth. Add to the fish with the mashed potatoes, parsley, 1 tablespoon of the flour, and pepper to taste. Add the egg yolk and mix well. If the mixture is a little dry, add some of the poaching milk; if too wet, add a little more flour.

3 Divide the mixture into 12 portions and shape each portion into a cake. Put the beaten eggs, remaining flour, and the breadcrumbs on 3 separate plates. Roll each fishcake in the flour, then in the beaten egg, and then in the breadcrumbs to coat.

4 Heat the oil in a nonstick baking sheet with a rim in the preheated oven for 5 minutes. Add the fishcakes and bake for 10 minutes, then carefully turn the fishcakes over and bake for an additional 10 minutes. Serve hot.

WINTER VEGETABLE COBBLER

SERVES 4

1 tbsp olive oil
1 garlic clove, crushed
8 small onions, halved
2 celery stalks, sliced
8 oz/225 g rutabaga, chopped
2 carrots, sliced
½ small head of cauliflower, broken into
  florets
8 oz/225 g button mushrooms, sliced
14 oz/400 g canned chopped tomatoes
¼ cup red lentils, rinsed
2 tbsp cornstarch
3–4 tbsp water

1¼ cups vegetable stock
2 tsp Tabasco sauce
2 tsp chopped fresh oregano
fresh oregano sprigs, for garnish

for the topping
heaping 1½ cups self-rising flour
pinch of salt
4 tbsp butter
scant 1¼ cups grated sharp Cheddar
  cheese
2 tsp chopped fresh oregano
1 egg, lightly beaten
⅔ cup milk

GRANDMA'S TIPS

This rib-sticking dish is just the thing for those cold winter evenings. The vegetables can be varied according to taste and season. You can make a curry-flavored cobbler by using curry paste instead of the Tabasco sauce. The topping can be made with whole wheat flour instead of white to make it more healthful.

1 Preheat the oven to 350°F/180°C. Heat the oil in a large skillet and cook the garlic and onions over low heat for 5 minutes. Add the celery, rutabaga, carrots, and cauliflower and cook for 2–3 minutes.

2 Add the mushrooms, tomatoes, and lentils. Place the cornstarch and water in a bowl and mix to make a smooth paste. Stir into the skillet with the stock, Tabasco, and oregano. Transfer to an ovenproof dish, cover, and bake in the preheated oven for 20 minutes.

3 To make the topping, sift the flour and salt into a bowl. Rub in the butter, then stir in most of the cheese and the chopped oregano. Beat the egg with the milk in a small bowl and add enough to the dry ingredients to make a soft dough. Knead, then roll out to ½ inch/1 cm thick and cut into 2-inch/5-cm circles.

4 Remove the dish from the oven and increase the temperature to 400°F/200°C. Arrange the dough circles around the edge of the dish, brush with the remaining egg and milk mixture, and sprinkle with the reserved cheese. Cook for an additional 10–12 minutes. Garnish with oregano sprigs and serve.

ROASTED BUTTERNUT
SQUASH RISOTTO

SERVES 4

1 lb 5 oz/600 g butternut squash or
  pumpkin, peeled and cut into bite-size
  pieces
4 tbsp olive oil
1 tsp honey
2 tbsp fresh basil, plus extra sprigs
  for garnish

2 tbsp fresh oregano
1 tbsp margarine
2 onions, finely chopped
1 lb/450 g risotto rice
¾ cup dry white wine
5 cups vegetable stock
salt and pepper

1 Preheat the oven to 400°F/200°C. Put the squash into a roasting pan. Mix
1 tablespoon of the oil with the honey and spoon over the squash. Turn the squash to
coat it in the mixture. Roast in the preheated oven for 30–35 minutes, or until tender.

2 Meanwhile, put the basil and oregano into a food processor with 2 tablespoons of the
remaining oil and process until finely chopped and blended. Set aside.

3 Heat the margarine and remaining oil in a large, heavy-bottom pan over medium heat.
Add the onions and cook, stirring occasionally, for 8 minutes, or until soft and golden.
Add the rice and cook for 2 minutes, stirring to coat the grains in the oil mixture.

4 Pour in the wine and bring to a boil. Reduce the heat slightly and cook until the wine
is almost absorbed. Add the stock, a little at a time, and cook over medium-low heat,
stirring constantly, for 20 minutes.

5 Gently stir in the herb oil and squash until thoroughly mixed into the rice and cook for
an additional 5 minutes, or until the rice is creamy and cooked but retaining a little bite in
the center of the grain. Season well with salt and pepper before serving, garnished with
sprigs of basil.

MACARONI & CHEESE

SERVES 4
2½ cups milk
1 onion, peeled
8 peppercorns
1 bay leaf
4 tbsp butter
scant ⅓ cup all-purpose flour
½ tsp ground nutmeg

⅓ cup heavy cream
pepper
3½ oz/100 g sharp Cheddar cheese, grated
3½ oz/100 g Roquefort cheese, crumbled
12 oz/350 g dried macaroni
3½ oz/100 g Gruyère or Emmental cheese, grated

GRANDMA'S TIPS

Macaroni & Cheese is a great family favorite. This rich version using three varieties of cheese can be made simpler using one cheese, such as Cheddar, and omitting the cream. You can also add some vegetables—steamed broccoli florets or baby spinach leaves will add extra color and nutrition.

1 Put the milk, onion, peppercorns, and bay leaf in a pan and bring to a boil. Remove from the heat and let stand for 15 minutes.

2 Melt the butter in a pan and stir in the flour until well combined and smooth. Cook over medium heat, stirring constantly, for 1 minute. Remove from the heat. Strain the milk to remove the solids and stir a little into the butter and flour mixture until well incorporated. Return to the heat and gradually add the remaining milk, stirring constantly, until it has all been incorporated. Cook for an additional 3 minutes, or until the sauce is smooth and thickened, then add the nutmeg, cream, and pepper to taste. Add the Cheddar and Roquefort cheeses and stir until melted.

3 Meanwhile, bring a large pan of water to a boil. Add the macaroni, then return to a boil and cook for 8–10 minutes, or until just tender. Drain well and add to the cheese sauce. Stir well together.

4 Preheat the broiler to high. Spoon the mixture into an ovenproof serving dish, then scatter over the Gruyère cheese and cook under the broiler until bubbling and brown.

STUFFED BAKED
POTATOES

SERVES 4
2 baking potatoes, scrubbed
1 tbsp olive oil
2 tbsp whole milk
2 tbsp butter
1 oz/25 g Cheddar or Gruyère cheese, grated

1 large egg, separated
salt and pepper
2 slices ham, cooked turkey, or unsmoked bacon, chopped
2 tbsp finely grated Parmesan cheese
salad, for serving

GRANDMA'S TIPS

Baked potatoes make for a perfect meal, particularly when they are stuffed with lots of tasty ingredients such as bolognese or chili sauce, flaked fish, or ratatouille—whatever you like. Make sure the potatoes are baked through so that they're soft inside and the skins are firm and crisp, which makes them most delicious. You can even rub salt into the skins with the oil to enhance the flavor.

1 Preheat the oven to 400°F/200°C. Prick the potatoes with a fork. Rub the oil all over the potatoes, place on a baking sheet, and bake in the preheated oven for 1 hour, or until the flesh is soft.

2 Remove the potatoes from the oven, cut in half lengthwise, and carefully scoop out the flesh into a bowl, keeping the skins intact. Set the skins aside.

3 Add the milk, butter, Cheddar cheese, and egg yolk to the potato and mash well. Season to taste with salt and pepper. Mix in the ham.

4 In a separate, grease-free bowl, whisk the egg white until stiff, then fold into the potato mixture.

5 Pile the potato mixture back into the skins and sprinkle over the Parmesan cheese. Return to the oven and bake for 20 minutes. Serve with salad.

MASHED POTATOES

SERVES 4

2 lb/900 g starchy potatoes, such as russet

4 tbsp butter
3 tbsp hot milk
salt and pepper

1 Peel the potatoes, placing them in cold water as you prepare the others to prevent them from turning brown.

2 Cut the potatoes into even-size chunks and cook in a large saucepan of boiling water over medium heat, covered, for 20–25 minutes until they are tender. Test with the point of a knife, but make sure you test right in the middle to avoid lumps.

3 Remove the pan from the heat and drain the potatoes. Return the potatoes to the hot pan and mash with a potato masher until smooth.

4 Add the butter and continue to mash until it is all mixed in, then add the milk (it is better hot because the potatoes absorb it more quickly to produce a creamier mash).

5 Taste the mashed potatoes and season with salt and pepper as necessary. Serve immediately.

BOSTON BEANS

SERVES 8
1 lb 2 oz/500 g dried great Northern
   beans, soaked overnight
2 onions, chopped
12 oz/350 g salt pork, diced

2 large tomatoes, peeled and chopped
2 tsp mustard
2 tbsp molasses
salt and pepper

GRANDMA'S TIPS

*A quick version can be made
using canned beans, which take
no time to cook; drain and rinse
them well before using. You can
use bacon strips or frankfurters
instead of the salt pork. Serve
as an accompaniment to chicken
drumsticks or pork spareribs for
a filling meal.*

1 Preheat the oven to 275°F/140°C. Drain the beans, rinse under cold running water,
and place in a large pan. Add enough cold water to cover, bring to a boil, then reduce
the heat and simmer for 15 minutes. Drain, reserving 1¼ cups of the cooking liquid.
Transfer the beans to a large casserole and add the onions and salt pork.

2 Return the reserved cooking liquid to the pan and add the tomatoes. Bring to a boil,
then reduce the heat and simmer for 10 minutes. Remove from the heat, stir in the
mustard and molasses, and season to taste with salt and pepper.

3 Pour the mixture into the casserole and bake in the preheated oven for 5 hours. Serve
hot.

Grandmas in this day and age are jetting off or cruising all over the world. Travel is cheaper and easier than in the past, making it possible to visit far-off destinations with diverse cultures and foods. Countries like China, Mexico, and the newly accessible Eastern European nations have all contributed to our varied cuisine. We have taken recipes from many different cultures and adapted them to our own way of eating. And as our society becomes increasingly multiethnic, ingredients for these types of recipes are becoming more

GRANDMA'S TRAVELS

readily available, not just from specialty shops but increasingly from mainstream supermarkets. Pasta has long been a favorite, and spaghetti bolognese is popular with adults and children alike. Pizza is an ideal finger food that can be made from scratch or using a prepared pizza shell, and it can then be topped with different ingredients so that everyone can choose their own. From farther afield come chicken Kiev and beef goulash, together with chicken fajitas and chili con carne, introducing new flavors and spices into our diets. Chow mein and Asian-style spareribs, with their use of Eastern spices and flavors, are also included in this chapter.

SPAGHETTI BOLOGNESE

SERVES 4

1 tbsp olive oil
1 onion, finely chopped
2 garlic cloves, chopped
1 carrot, chopped
1 celery stalk, chopped
¼ cup pancetta or lean bacon, diced
1 ½ cups lean ground beef

14 oz/400 g canned chopped tomatoes
2 tsp dried oregano
½ cup red wine
2 tbsp tomato paste
salt and pepper
12 oz/350 g dried spaghetti
freshly grated Parmesan cheese,
 for serving (optional)

GRANDMA'S TIPS

This is the world's favorite spaghetti dish, loved by adults and children alike. A good sauce takes time to make, but is worth the effort. Prepare double quantities and freeze in individual portions so that you always have some on hand for a quick meal. Some recipes add chicken livers or mushrooms— the choice is up to you. Serve this dish piping hot with lots of grated cheese.

1 Heat the oil in a large skillet over a high heat. Add the onions and cook for 3 minutes.

2 Add the garlic, carrot, celery, and pancetta, and cook for about 3–4 minutes, or until just starting to brown.

3 Add the beef and cook over a high heat for 3 minutes, or until the meat has browned.

4 Stir in the tomatoes, oregano, and red wine and bring to a boil over a high heat. Reduce the heat and simmer for about 45 minutes.

5 Stir in the tomato paste and season with salt and pepper.

6 Bring a pan of lightly salted water to a boil over a medium heat. Add the pasta and cook for about 8–10 minutes, until tender but still firm to the bite. Drain.

7 Transfer the pasta to 4 serving plates and pour over the sauce. Toss to mix well and serve with Parmesan cheese, if you wish.

SPAGHETTI WITH MEATBALLS

SERVES 6
1 potato, diced
salt and pepper
1 ¾ cups ground beef
1 onion, finely chopped
1 egg
4 tbsp chopped fresh flat-leaf parsley
all-purpose flour, for dusting

5 tbsp virgin olive oil
1 ¾ cups strained tomatoes
2 tbsp tomato paste
1 lb/450 g dried spaghetti

for garnish
6 fresh basil leaves, shredded
Parmesan cheese shavings

1 Place the potato in a small pan, add cold water to cover and a pinch of salt, and bring to a boil. Cook for 10–15 minutes, until tender, then drain. Either mash thoroughly with a potato masher or fork or pass through a potato ricer.

2 Combine the potato, ground beef, onion, egg, and parsley in a bowl and season to taste with salt and pepper. Spread out the flour on a plate. With dampened hands, shape the meat mixture into walnut-size balls and roll in the flour. Shake off any excess.

3 Heat the oil in a heavy-bottom skillet, add the meatballs, and cook over medium heat, stirring and turning frequently, for 8–10 minutes, until golden all over.

4 Add the strained tomatoes and tomato paste and cook for an additional 10 minutes, until the sauce is reduced and thickened.

5 Meanwhile, bring a large pan of lightly salted water to a boil. Add the pasta, bring back to a boil, and cook for 8–10 minutes, until tender but still firm to the bite.

6 Drain well and add to the meatball sauce, tossing well to coat. Transfer to a warmed serving dish, garnish with the basil leaves and Parmesan, and serve immediately.

FETTUCCINE ALFREDO

SERVES 4
2 tbsp butter
scant 1 cup heavy cream
1 lb/450 g fresh fettuccine
1 cup freshly grated Parmesan cheese,
  plus extra for serving

pinch of freshly grated nutmeg
salt and pepper
fresh flat-leaf parsley sprigs, for garnish

1 Put the butter and $2/3$ cup of the cream in a large pan and bring the mixture to a boil over medium heat. Reduce the heat, then simmer gently for about $1^1/2$ minutes, or until the cream has thickened slightly.

2 Meanwhile, bring a large pan of lightly salted water to a boil over medium heat. Add the pasta and cook for about 2–3 minutes, or until done. Drain the pasta thoroughly and return to the pan, then pour over the cream sauce.

3 Toss the pasta in the sauce over low heat until thoroughly coated.

4 Add the remaining cream, Parmesan cheese, and nutmeg to the pasta mixture, and season to taste with salt and pepper. Toss the pasta thoroughly in the mixture while gently heating through.

5 Transfer the pasta mixture to warmed serving bowls and garnish with a fresh parsley sprig. Serve immediately, handing extra grated Parmesan cheese separately.

LASAGNA

SERVES 4
2 tbsp olive oil
2 oz/55 g pancetta or rindless lean
   bacon, chopped
1 onion, chopped
1 garlic clove, finely chopped
1 cup fresh ground beef
2 celery stalks, chopped
2 carrots, chopped
salt and pepper
pinch of sugar
½ tsp dried oregano
14 oz/400 g canned chopped tomatoes
8 oz/225 g dried no-cook lasagna noodles
1 cup freshly grated Parmesan cheese,
   plus extra for sprinkling

for the cheese sauce
1¼ cups milk
1 bay leaf
6 black peppercorns
slice of onion
blade of mace
2 tbsp butter
3 tbsp all-purpose flour
2 tsp Dijon mustard
2½ oz/70 g Cheddar cheese, grated
2½ oz/70 g Gruyère cheese, grated
salt and pepper

GRANDMA'S TIPS

This dish is quite complicated to make, as it requires you to make both a meat and a cheese sauce. To cheat a little, you can buy a prepared cheese sauce to cut down on the preparation time. Make sure you use no-cook lasagna noodles as they will not need to be boiled before use.

1 Preheat the oven to 375°F/190°C. Heat the olive oil in a large, heavy-bottom pan. Add the pancetta and cook over medium heat, stirring occasionally, for 3 minutes, or until the fat starts to run. Add the onion and garlic and cook, stirring occasionally, for 5 minutes, or until softened.

2 Add the beef and cook, breaking it up with a wooden spoon, until browned all over. Stir in the celery and carrot and cook for 5 minutes. Season to taste with salt and pepper. Add the sugar, oregano, and tomatoes. Bring to a boil, reduce the heat, and let simmer for 30 minutes.

3 Meanwhile, make the cheese sauce. Pour the milk into a saucepan and add the bay leaf, peppercorns, onion, and mace. Heat gently to just below the boiling point, then remove from the heat, cover, and leave to infuse for 10 minutes. Strain the milk into a pitcher. Melt the butter in a separate saucepan. Sprinkle in the flour and cook over low heat, stirring constantly, for 1 minute. Remove from the heat and gradually stir in the warm milk. Return to the heat and bring to a boil, stirring. Cook, stirring, until thickened and smooth. Stir in the mustard and both cheeses, then season to taste with salt and pepper.

4 In a large, rectangular ovenproof dish, make alternate layers of meat sauce, lasagna noodles, and Parmesan cheese. Pour the cheese sauce over the layers, covering them completely, and sprinkle with Parmesan cheese. Bake in the preheated oven for 30 minutes, or until golden brown and bubbling. Serve immediately.

CHEESE & TOMATO
PIZZA

SERVES 4
for the pizza dough
½ oz/15 g active dry yeast
1 tsp sugar
1 cup warm water
2¾ cups bread flour, plus extra
 for dusting
1 tsp salt
1 tbsp olive oil, plus extra for oiling

for the topping
14 oz/400 g canned chopped tomatoes
2 garlic cloves, crushed
2 tsp dried basil
1 tbsp olive oil
salt and pepper
2 tbsp tomato paste
3½ oz/100 g mozzarella cheese, chopped
2 tbsp freshly grated Parmesan cheese

GRANDMA'S TIPS

Nowadays pizza is served with all sorts of toppings—lots of them quite bizarre. This is a basic recipe that can be adapted to personal choice. Olives, both black and green, anchovy fillets, sliced mushrooms, and salami all work well and add lots of color and texture. Ready-made pizza shells are widely available and can be the base for a quickly assembled dish. Family members can make their own individual pizzas using their favorite toppings.

1 Place the yeast and sugar in a measuring cup and mix with 4 tbsp of the water. Leave the yeast mixture in a warm place for 15 minutes or until frothy.

2 Mix the flour with the salt and make a well in the center. Add the oil, the yeast mixture, and the remaining water. Using a wooden spoon, mix to form a smooth dough.

3 Turn the dough out onto a floured surface and knead for 4–5 minutes or until smooth.

4 Return the dough to the bowl, cover with an oiled sheet of plastic wrap and leave to rise for 30 minutes or until doubled in size.

5 Knead the dough for 2 minutes. Stretch the dough with your hands, then place it on an oiled cookie sheet or pizza pan, pushing out the edges until even. The dough should be no more than ¼ inch/6 mm thick because it will rise during cooking.

6 Preheat the oven to 400°F/200°C. To make the topping, place the tomatoes, garlic, dried basil, olive oil, and salt and pepper to taste in a large skillet and leave to simmer for 20 minutes or until the sauce has thickened. Stir in the tomato paste and leave to cool slightly.

7 Spread the topping evenly over the pizza base. Top with the mozzarella and Parmesan cheeses and bake in the preheated oven for 20–25 minutes. Serve hot.

RATATOUILLE

SERVES 4
2 eggplants
4 zucchini
2 yellow bell peppers
2 red bell peppers
2 onions

2 garlic cloves
⅔ cup olive oil
1 bouquet garni
3 large tomatoes, peeled, seeded, and
    coarsely chopped
salt and pepper

1 Roughly chop the eggplants and zucchini, and seed and chop the bell peppers. Slice the onions and finely chop the garlic. Heat the oil in a large pan. Add the onions and cook over low heat, stirring occasionally, for 5 minutes, or until softened. Add the garlic and cook, stirring frequently for an additional 2 minutes.

2 Add the eggplants, zucchini, and bell peppers. Increase the heat to medium and cook, stirring occasionally, until the bell peppers begin to color. Add the bouquet garni, reduce the heat, cover, and simmer gently for 40 minutes.

3 Stir in the chopped tomatoes and season to taste with salt and pepper. Re-cover the pan and simmer gently for an additional 10 minutes. Remove and discard the bouquet garni. Serve warm or cold.

PAELLA

SERVES 4–6

5¼ cups fish stock or water
12 large raw shrimp, in their shells
½ tsp saffron threads
2 tbsp hot water
3½ oz/100 g skinless, boneless chicken breast, cut into ½-inch/1-cm pieces
3½ oz/100 g pork tenderloin, cut into ½-inch/1-cm pieces
salt and pepper
3 tbsp olive oil
3½ oz/100 g Spanish chorizo sausage, casing removed, cut into ½-inch/1-cm slices

1 large red onion, chopped
2 garlic cloves, crushed
½ tsp cayenne pepper
½ tsp paprika
1 red bell pepper, seeded and sliced
1 green bell pepper, seeded and sliced
12 cherry tomatoes, halved
1½ cups medium-grain paella rice
1 tbsp chopped fresh parsley
2 tsp chopped fresh tarragon

GRANDMA'S TIPS

This traditional Spanish dish includes lots of ingredients, which is wonderful for a large party, but a simpler paella can be made using just chicken and shrimp and is great for everyday meals. Double the chicken and shrimp in the recipe, and buy precooked shrimp to save time. Follow the directions here, adding or omitting any vegetables as you wish.

1 Put the stock in a large pan and bring to a simmer. Add the shrimp and cook for 2 minutes. Using a slotted spoon, transfer the shrimp to a bowl and set aside. Let the stock simmer. Put the saffron threads and water in a small bowl or cup and let infuse for a few minutes.

2 Season the chicken and pork to taste with salt and pepper. Heat the oil in a paella pan or wide, shallow skillet and cook the chicken, pork, and chorizo over medium heat, stirring, for 5 minutes, or until golden. Add the onion and cook, stirring, for 2–3 minutes, or until softened. Add the garlic, cayenne pepper, paprika, and saffron and its soaking liquid and cook, stirring constantly, for 1 minute. Add the bell pepper slices and tomato halves and cook, stirring, for an additional 2 minutes.

3 Add the rice and herbs and cook, stirring constantly, for 1 minute, or until the rice is glossy and coated. Pour in about 5 cups of the hot stock and bring to a boil. Reduce the heat and let simmer, uncovered, for 10 minutes. Do not stir during cooking, but shake the pan once or twice. Season to taste with salt and pepper, then shake the pan and cook for an additional 10 minutes, or until the rice grains are plump and almost cooked. If the liquid is absorbed too quickly, pour in a little more hot stock, then shake the pan to spread the liquid through the paella. Do not stir it in. Add the shrimp and shake the pan, but do not stir. Cook for an additional 2 minutes.

4 When all the liquid has been absorbed and you detect a faint toasty aroma coming from the rice, remove from the heat immediately to prevent burning. Cover the pan with a clean dish towel or foil and let stand for 5 minutes. Divide the paella among warmed serving plates and serve immediately.

COQ AU VIN

SERVES 4
4 tbsp butter
2 tbsp olive oil
4 lb/1.8 kg chicken pieces
4 oz/115 g rindless smoked bacon,
    cut into strips
4 oz/115 g pearl onions
4 oz/115 g cremini mushrooms, halved

2 garlic cloves, finely chopped
2 tbsp brandy
1 cup red wine
1¼ cups chicken stock
1 bouquet garni
salt and pepper
2 tbsp all-purpose flour
bay leaves, for garnish

GRANDMA'S TIPS

Coq au vin is usually made with red wine, but it also can be made with a white wine, such as a Riesling. If you're using white wine, add 1 cup of light cream before serving and garnish with freshly chopped parsley.

1 Melt half the butter with the olive oil in a large, flameproof casserole. Add the chicken and cook over medium heat, stirring, for 8–10 minutes, or until golden brown. Add the bacon, onions, mushrooms, and garlic.

2 Pour in the brandy and set it aflame with a match or taper. When the flames have died down, add the wine, stock, and bouquet garni and season to taste with salt and pepper. Bring to a boil, reduce the heat, and simmer gently for 1 hour, or until the chicken pieces are cooked through and tender. Meanwhile, make a beurre manié by mashing the remaining butter with the flour in a small bowl.

3 Remove and discard the bouquet garni. Transfer the chicken to a large plate and keep warm. Stir the beurre manié into the casserole, a little at a time. Bring to a boil, return the chicken to the casserole, and serve immediately, garnished with bay leaves.

BEEF BOURGUIGNON

SERVES 4–6

6 tbsp butter
2 tbsp corn oil
²⁄₃ cup smoked lardons, blanched for 30
    seconds, then drained and patted dry
2 lb/900 g braising beef, such as chuck
    or leg
2 large garlic cloves, crushed
1 carrot, diced
1 leek, halved and sliced
1 onion, finely chopped

2 tbsp all-purpose flour
salt and pepper
1 ½ cups full-bodied red wine
about 2 cups beef stock
1 tbsp tomato paste
1 bouquet garni
12 pearl onions, peeled but kept whole
12 button mushrooms
chopped fresh flat-leaf parsley, for garnish
French bread, for serving

1 Preheat the oven to 300°F/150°C. Heat 2 tablespoons of the butter and 1 tablespoon of the oil in a large, flameproof casserole. Cook the lardons over medium-high heat, stirring, for 2 minutes, or until beginning to brown. Using a slotted spoon, remove from the casserole and drain on paper towels.

2 Trim the beef and cut it into 2-inch/5-cm chunks. Add the beef to the casserole and cook over high heat, stirring frequently, for 5 minutes, or until browned on all sides and sealed, adding more of the butter or oil to the casserole as necessary. Using a slotted spoon, transfer the beef to a plate.

3 Pour off all but 2 tablespoons of the fat from the casserole. Add the garlic, carrot, leek, and chopped onion and cook over medium heat, stirring frequently, for 3 minutes, or until the onion is beginning to soften. Sprinkle in the flour, season to taste with salt and pepper, and cook, stirring constantly, for 2 minutes, then remove the casserole from the heat.

4 Gradually stir in the wine and stock and add the tomato paste and bouquet garni, then return to the heat and bring to a boil, stirring and scraping any sediment from the bottom of the casserole.

5 Return the beef and lardons to the casserole and add extra stock if necessary so that the ingredients are covered by about ½ inch/1 cm of liquid. Slowly return to a boil, then cover and cook in the preheated oven for 2 hours.

6 Meanwhile, heat 2 tablespoons of the remaining butter and the remaining oil in a large sauté pan or skillet and cook the pearl onions over medium-high heat, stirring frequently, until golden all over. Using a slotted spoon, transfer the onions to a plate.

7 Heat the remaining butter in the pan and cook the mushrooms, stirring frequently, until golden brown. Remove from the pan and then stir them, with the onions, into the casserole. Re-cover and cook for an additional 30 minutes, or until the beef is very tender.

8 Discard the bouquet garni, then adjust the seasoning to taste. Serve garnished with parsley, accompanied by plenty of French bread for mopping up all the juices.

CHILI CON CARNE

SERVES 4
1 tbsp sunflower or corn oil
1 small onion, coarsely chopped
1 or 2 garlic cloves, coarsely chopped
1 green bell pepper, seeded and diced
8 oz/225 g ground beef
1 tsp chili powder
14 oz/400 g canned chopped tomatoes

½ tsp salt (optional)
14 oz/400 g canned kidney beans,
  drained and rinsed

for serving
grated cheese
freshly cooked rice
tortilla chips

GRANDMA'S TIPS

Make sure to check the strength of your chili powder, as chili powder comes in different strengths. If you don't like your chili too hot, use a mild powder and decrease the amount. Sour cream and guacamole are traditional accompaniments.

1 Heat the oil in a shallow skillet over low heat. Stir in the onion, garlic, and green bell pepper and cook gently for 5 minutes.

2 Add the ground beef and stir well. Increase the heat to high and cook for 5 minutes, stirring occasionally. Spoon off any excess fat. Sprinkle over the chili powder and mix well. Continue cooking for 2–3 minutes. Stir in the tomatoes, reduce the heat, cover, and cook gently for at least 30 minutes. You may need to add a little water or beef stock if it starts to dry out.

3 Halfway through the cooking time check the seasoning and stir in the salt if needed. Add more chili powder to taste, but be careful not to use too much.

4 Add the drained kidney beans to the chili mixture 10–15 minutes before the end of the cooking time so that they heat through with the meat and spices.

5 Serve immediately topped with a little grated cheese and accompanied by freshly cooked rice and tortilla chips.

CHICKEN FAJITAS

SERVES 4
3 tbsp olive oil, plus extra for drizzling
3 tbsp maple syrup or honey
1 tbsp red wine vinegar
2 garlic cloves, crushed
2 tsp dried oregano
1–2 tsp dried red pepper flakes
salt and pepper
4 skinless, boneless chicken breasts
2 red bell peppers, seeded and cut into
   1-inch/2.5-cm strips
8 flour tortillas, warmed

GRANDMA'S TIPS

Tortillas can be heated by wrapping in foil and placing in a warm oven for 3–4 minutes. Your family will enjoy wrapping their own fajitas—provide bowls of shredded lettuce, salsa, and sour cream to choose from.

1 Place the oil, maple syrup, vinegar, garlic, oregano, pepper flakes, and salt and pepper to taste in a large, shallow dish or bowl and mix together.

2 Slice the chicken across the grain into slices 1 inch/2.5 cm thick. Toss in the marinade until well coated. Cover and let chill in the refrigerator for 2–3 hours, turning occasionally.

3 Heat a grill pan until hot. Lift the chicken slices from the marinade with a slotted spoon, lay on the grill pan, and cook over medium-high heat for 3–4 minutes on each side, or until cooked through. Remove the chicken to a warmed serving plate and keep warm.

4 Add the bell peppers, skin-side down, to the grill pan and cook for 2 minutes on each side. Transfer to the serving plate.

5 Serve at once with the warmed tortillas to be used as wraps.

NACHOS

SERVES 6

6 oz/175 g tortilla chips
14 oz/400 g canned refried beans, warmed
2 tbsp finely chopped jarred jalapeño chiles

7 oz/200 g canned or jarred pimentos or roasted bell peppers, drained and finely sliced
salt and pepper
4 oz/115 g Gruyère cheese, grated
4 oz/115 g Cheddar cheese, grated

1 Preheat the oven to 400°F/200°C.

2 Spread the tortilla chips out over the bottom of a large, shallow, ovenproof dish or roasting pan. Cover with the warmed refried beans. Sprinkle over the chiles and pimentos and season to taste with salt and pepper. Mix the cheeses together in a bowl and sprinkle on top.

3 Bake in the preheated oven for 5–8 minutes, or until the cheese is bubbling and melted. Serve at once.

BEEF ENCHILADAS

SERVES 4
2 tbsp olive oil, plus extra for oiling
2 large onions, thinly sliced
1 lb 4 oz/550 g lean beef, cut into
  bite-size pieces
1 tbsp ground cumin
½–1 tsp cayenne pepper
1 tsp paprika
salt and pepper
8 soft corn tortillas
8 oz/225 g Cheddar cheese, grated

for the taco sauce
1 tbsp olive oil
1 onion, finely chopped
1 green bell pepper, seeded and diced
1–2 fresh hot green chiles, seeded and
  finely chopped
3 garlic cloves, crushed
1 tsp ground cumin
1 tsp ground coriander
1 tsp brown sugar
1 lb/450 g ripe tomatoes, peeled and
  chopped
juice of ½ lemon
salt and pepper

GRANDMA'S TIPS

*Another use for soft tortillas—
here they are used like pancakes,
stuffed with meat sauce, rolled
up, covered with the remaining
sauce and grated cheese, and then
baked. If you are cooking for
children, use the spices sparingly.
This recipe can also be made
with ground lamb or chicken.*

1 Preheat the oven to 350°F/180°C. Oil a large, rectangular baking dish.

2 To make the taco sauce, heat the oil in a deep skillet over medium heat. Add the onion and cook for 5 minutes, or until softened. Add the bell pepper and chiles and cook for 5 minutes. Add the garlic, cumin, coriander, and sugar and cook the sauce for an additional 2 minutes, stirring. Add the tomatoes, lemon juice, and salt and pepper to taste. Bring to a boil, then reduce the heat and let simmer for 10 minutes. Remove from the heat and set aside.

3 Heat the oil in a large skillet over low heat. Add the onions and cook for 10 minutes, or until soft. Remove with a slotted spoon and set aside. Increase the heat to high, add the beef, and cook, stirring, for 2–3 minutes until browned all over. Reduce the heat to medium, add the spices and salt and pepper to taste, and cook, stirring constantly, for 2 minutes.

4 Warm each tortilla in a lightly oiled nonstick skillet for 15 seconds on each side, then dip each in the taco sauce. Top each with some of the beef and onion mixture and a little grated cheese and roll up. Place seam-side down in the prepared baking dish, top with the remaining taco sauce and grated cheese, and bake in the oven for 30 minutes.

CHICKEN KIEV

SERVES 4
4 tbsp butter, softened
I garlic clove, finely chopped
I tbsp finely chopped fresh parsley,
  plus extra sprigs for garnish
I tbsp finely chopped fresh oregano
salt and pepper
4 skinless, boneless chicken breasts
I ¾ cups fresh white or whole wheat
  breadcrumbs

3 tbsp freshly grated Parmesan cheese
I egg, beaten
I cup vegetable oil, for
  deep-frying

for serving
freshly cooked new potatoes
selection of cooked vegetables

GRANDMA'S TIPS
*Chill the herb butter well before
using it so it won't melt too
quickly during cooking. Sautéed
sliced mushrooms or sun-dried
tomatoes can be added to the
butter for an interesting twist.*

1 Place the butter and garlic in a bowl and mix together well. Stir in the chopped herbs and season well with salt and pepper. Pound the chicken breasts to flatten them to an even thickness, then place a tablespoon of the herb butter in the center of each one. Fold in the sides to enclose the butter, then secure with toothpicks.

2 Combine the breadcrumbs and grated Parmesan on a plate. Dip the chicken parcels into the beaten egg, then coat in the breadcrumb mixture. Transfer to a plate, cover, and chill for 30 minutes. Remove from the refrigerator and coat in the egg and then the breadcrumb mixture for a second time.

3 Pour the oil into a deep-fat fryer to a depth that will cover the chicken parcels. Heat until it reaches 350–375°F/180–190°C, or until a cube of bread browns in 30 seconds. Transfer the chicken to the hot oil and deep-fry for 5 minutes, or until cooked through. Lift out the chicken and drain on paper towels.

4 Divide the chicken among 4 serving plates, garnish with parsley sprigs, and serve with new potatoes and a selection of vegetables.

BEEF GOULASH

SERVES 4

2 tbsp vegetable oil
1 large onion, chopped
1 garlic clove, crushed
1 lb 10 oz/750 g lean braising beef
2 tbsp paprika
14 oz/400 g canned chopped tomatoes
2 tbsp tomato paste
1 large red bell pepper, seeded and
   chopped

6 oz/175 g button mushrooms, sliced
2½ cups beef stock
1 tbsp cornstarch
1 tbsp water
salt and pepper
chopped fresh parsley, for garnish
freshly cooked long-grain and wild rice,
   for serving

1 Heat the vegetable oil in a large, heavy-bottom skillet. Add the onion and garlic and cook over low heat for 3–4 minutes.

2 Using a sharp knife, cut the beef into chunks, add to the skillet, and cook over high heat for 3 minutes, or until browned. Add the paprika and stir well, then add the tomatoes, tomato paste, bell pepper, and mushrooms. Cook for an additional 2 minutes, stirring frequently. Pour in the stock. Bring to a boil, reduce the heat, cover, and simmer for 1½–2 hours, or until the meat is tender.

3 Blend the cornstarch and water together in a small bowl, then add to the skillet, stirring, until thickened and smooth. Cook for 1 minute. Season to taste with salt and pepper.

4 Transfer the beef goulash to a warmed serving dish, garnish with chopped fresh parsley, and serve with a mix of long-grain and wild rice.

MUSHROOM
STROGANOFF

SERVES 4

1 lb 4 oz/550 g mixed fresh mushrooms,
   such as cremini, cèpes, and oyster
1 red onion, diced
2 garlic cloves, crushed
2 cups vegetable stock
1 tbsp tomato paste
2 tbsp lemon juice

1 tbsp cornstarch
2 tbsp cold water
½ cup lowfat plain yogurt
3 tbsp chopped fresh parsley
freshly ground black pepper
freshly cooked brown or white rice,
   for serving

GRANDMA'S TIPS

This is a vegetarian version of the traditional beef stroganoff. Extra sour cream and a dash of paprika make a colorful and tasty garnish.

1 Put the mushrooms, onion, garlic, stock, tomato paste, and lemon juice into a pan and bring to a boil. Reduce the heat, cover, and let simmer for 15 minutes, or until the onion is tender.

2 Blend the cornstarch with the water in a small bowl and stir into the mushroom mixture. Return to a boil, stirring constantly, and cook until the sauce thickens. Reduce the heat and let simmer for an additional 2–3 minutes, stirring occasionally.

3 Just before serving, remove the pan from the heat, and stir in the yogurt, making sure that the stroganoff is not boiling or it may separate and curdle. Stir in 2 tablespoons of the parsley and season to taste with pepper. Transfer the stroganoff to a warmed serving dish, sprinkle over the remaining parsley, and serve immediately with freshly cooked brown or white rice.

SWEET & SOUR SHRIMP

SERVES 4

1 lb/450 g cooked jumbo shrimp
1 tbsp peanut or corn oil
4 scallions, finely chopped
2 tsp finely chopped fresh ginger
2 tbsp dark soy sauce
2 tbsp brown sugar
3 tbsp rice vinegar

1 tbsp Chinese rice wine
½ cup fish or chicken stock
1 tsp cornstarch
1–2 tbsp water
dash of sesame oil
shredded Napa cabbage, for serving
shredded scallions, for garnish

GRANDMA'S TIPS

For a change, try making this dish with pork tenderloin instead of shrimp. Finely slice the pork into medallions and fry in the wok or skillet, turning occasionally until cooked through. Then add the other ingredients as the recipe directs.

1 Peel and devein the shrimp, pat dry with paper towels, and reserve.

2 Heat the oil in a preheated wok or large skillet. Add the scallions and ginger and stir-fry over high heat for 1 minute. Add the soy sauce, sugar, vinegar, rice wine, and stock and bring to a boil.

3 Place the cornstarch and water in a small bowl and mix to make a paste. Stir 1 tablespoon of the paste into the sauce and add the shrimp. Cook, stirring, until slightly thickened and smooth. Sprinkle with sesame oil.

4 Make a bed of Napa cabbage leaves in 4 serving bowls and top with shrimp and sauce. Garnish with the shredded scallions and serve immediately.

PORK CHOW MEIN

SERVES 4

9 oz/250 g egg noodles
4–5 tbsp vegetable oil
9 oz/250 g pork tenderloin, cooked
4½ oz/125 g green beans
2 tbsp light soy sauce

1 tsp salt
½ tsp sugar
1 tbsp Chinese rice wine or dry sherry
2 scallions, finely shredded
a few drops sesame oil
chili sauce, for serving (optional)

1 Cook the noodles in boiling water according to the instructions on the packet, then drain and rinse under cold water. Drain again then toss with 1 tablespoon of the oil.

2 Slice the pork into thin shreds and trim the beans.

3 Heat 3 tablespoons of the oil in a preheated wok until hot. Add the noodles and stir-fry for 2–3 minutes with 1 tablespoon of the soy sauce, then remove to a serving dish. Keep warm.

4 Heat the remaining oil and stir-fry the beans and meat for 2 minutes. Add the salt, sugar, rice wine, the remaining soy sauce, and about half of the scallions to the wok.

5 Stir the mixture in the wok, adding a little stock if necessary, then pour on top of the noodles, and sprinkle with sesame oil and the remaining scallions.

6 Serve the chow mein hot or cold with chili sauce, if using.

ASIAN-STYLE
SPARERIBS

SERVES 4
2 lb 4 oz/1 kg pork spareribs, separated
4 tbsp dark soy sauce
3 tbsp brown sugar
1 tbsp peanut or sunflower oil

2 garlic cloves, finely chopped
2 tsp Chinese five-spice powder
½-inch/1-cm piece fresh ginger, grated
shredded scallions, for serving

GRANDMA'S TIPS

An easy way to marinate meat is to put it into a large zip-top plastic bag, pour in the marinade, seal the bag, and shake well. Refrigerate overnight. During the last 15 minutes of cooking do not baste with marinades that have been in contact with raw meat. To play it safe reserve a portion of the marinade for basting before marinating the spareribs.

1 Place the spareribs in a large, shallow, nonmetallic dish. Mix the soy sauce, sugar, oil, garlic, Chinese five-spice powder, and ginger together in a measuring cup. Pour the mixture over the ribs and turn until the ribs are well coated in the marinade.

2 Cover the dish with plastic wrap and let marinate in the refrigerator for at least 6 hours.

3 Preheat the barbecue. Drain the ribs, reserving the marinade. Cook over medium-hot coals, turning and brushing frequently with the reserved marinade, for 30–40 minutes. Transfer to a large serving dish, garnish with the shredded scallions, and serve immediately.

Christmas and other holidays were always when Grandma came into her own. She would love having her family around her and always pulled out all the stops to give them the best of everything. Appetizers of special soups and pâté are included in this chapter, and there are, of course, recipes for roast turkey and the all-important stuffing. Ham, goose, and beef recipes are also provided as alternatives to the turkey, but they work just as well for winter dinners—and the salmon dish is ideal for a summer's day, too.

GRANDMA'S FESTIVE FARE

Vegetarians won't be left out, as there is a mixed nut loaf topped with a cranberry and red wine sauce, and some delicious individual vegetable dishes are provided, too. Those with a sweet tooth will not be disappointed, as there are two very special classic pies to choose from—pumpkin and pecan. These recipes can be used at other times of the year as well to celebrate any festival in the calendar or a special family event like a birth, christening, or birthday.

MUSHROOM SOUP

SERVES 4
2 tbsp olive oil
1 onion, chopped
1 garlic clove, chopped
4½ oz/125 g sweet potato, peeled
  and chopped
1 leek, trimmed and sliced
7 oz/200 g cremini mushrooms
5½ oz/150 g wild mushrooms

2½ cups vegetable stock
1½ cups light cream
4 tbsp sherry
salt and pepper

for garnish/serving
Parmesan cheese shavings
sautéed sliced wild mushrooms
fresh crusty bread

GRANDMA'S TIPS

*When you can only find
cultivated mushrooms, increase
the flavor of the soup by adding
some dried porcini mushrooms.
Rehydrate the porcini in hot
water to cover for 15–20 minutes
and then add both the porcini
and their soaking liquid to the
soup.*

1 Heat the oil in a pan over medium heat. Add the onion and garlic and cook, stirring, for 3 minutes until softened slightly. Add the sweet potato and cook for another 3 minutes. Stir in the leek and cook for another 2 minutes.

2 Stir in the mushrooms, stock, and cream. Bring the mixture to a boil, then reduce the heat and simmer gently, stirring occasionally, for about 25 minutes. Remove from the heat, stir in the sherry, and let cool a little.

3 Transfer half of the soup into a food processor and blend until smooth. Return the mixture to the pan with the rest of the soup, season with salt and pepper and reheat gently, stirring. Pour into 4 warmed soup bowls, garnish with Parmesan shavings and wild mushrooms, and serve with fresh crusty bread.

PUMPKIN SOUP

SERVES 4
2 tbsp olive oil
1 onion, chopped
1 garlic clove, chopped
1 tbsp chopped fresh ginger
1 small red chile, seeded and finely
   chopped

2 tbsp chopped fresh cilantro
1 bay leaf
2 lb 4 oz/1 kg pumpkin, peeled, seeded,
   and diced
2½ cups vegetable stock
salt and pepper
light cream, for garnish

GRANDMA'S TIPS

Pumpkins are often tough-skinned and difficult to handle. The easiest way to prepare a pumpkin or squash is to cut it into quarters using a sharp knife, then remove the seeds and cut into smaller pieces. These pieces will then be easier to peel, either using a sharp knife or a potato peeler. Buying peeled and cut pumpkin from the supermarket makes things easier still.

1 Heat the oil in a pan over medium heat. Add the onion and garlic and cook, stirring, for about 4 minutes, until slightly softened. Add the ginger, chile, cilantro, bay leaf, and pumpkin, and cook for another 3 minutes.

2 Pour in the stock and bring to a boil. Using a slotted spoon, skim any foam from the surface. Reduce the heat and simmer gently, stirring occasionally, for about 25 minutes, or until the pumpkin is tender. Remove from the heat, take out the bay leaf, and let cool a little.

3 Transfer the soup into a food processor and blend until smooth (you may have to do this in batches). Return the mixture to the pan and season with salt and pepper. Reheat gently, stirring. Remove from the heat, pour into 4 warmed soup bowls, garnish each one with a swirl of cream, and serve.

CHICKEN LIVER PÂTÉ

SERVES 4–6

1 cup butter
8 oz/225 g trimmed chicken livers,
   thawed if frozen
2 tbsp Marsala or brandy
1½ tsp chopped fresh sage

1 garlic clove, coarsely chopped
⅔ cup heavy cream
salt and pepper
fresh bay leaves or sage leaves,
   for garnish
crackers, for serving

1 Melt 3 tablespoons of the butter in a large, heavy-bottom skillet. Add the chicken livers and cook over medium heat for about 4 minutes on each side. They should be browned on the outside but still pink in the middle. Transfer to a food processor and process until finely chopped.

2 Stir the Marsala or brandy into the skillet, scraping up any sediment with a wooden spoon, then add to the food processor with the sage, garlic, and ½ cup of the remaining butter. Process until smooth. Add the cream, season with salt and pepper, and process until thoroughly combined and smooth. Spoon the pâté into a dish or individual ramekins, level the surface, and let cool completely.

3 Melt the remaining butter, then spoon it over the surface of the pâté. Decorate with herb leaves, cool, then let chill in the refrigerator. Serve with crackers.

BLEU CHEESE & WALNUT TARTLETS

MAKES 12

for the pie dough
1½ cups all-purpose flour, plus extra
   for dusting
pinch of celery salt
3½ oz/100 g cold butter, cut into pieces,
   plus extra for greasing
¼ cup walnut halves, chopped in a food
   processor
cold water

for the filling
2 tbsp butter
2 celery stalks, trimmed and finely
   chopped
1 small leek, trimmed and finely chopped
scant 1 cup heavy cream, plus 2 tbsp
   extra
7 oz/200 g bleu cheese
salt and pepper
3 egg yolks

GRANDMA'S TIPS
*To make these delicious tartlets
more quickly you can use store-
bought pie pastry. The tartlets
won't have that walnut flavor
or texture, but the filling will be
just as tasty.*

1 Lightly grease a 3-inch/7.5-cm, 12-hole muffin pan. Sift the flour and celery salt into a food processor, add the butter, and process until the mixture resembles fine breadcrumbs. Transfer the mixture to a bowl and add the walnuts and a little cold water, just enough to bring the dough together. Turn out onto a floured counter and cut the dough in half. Roll out the first piece and cut out six 3½-inch/9-cm circles. Take each circle and roll out to 4½ inches/12 cm diameter and fit into the muffin holes, pressing to fill the holes. Do the same with the remaining dough. Put a piece of parchment paper in each hole, fill with dried beans, then put the pan in the refrigerator to chill for 30 minutes. Meanwhile, preheat the oven to 400°F/200°C.

2 Remove the muffin pan from the refrigerator and bake the tartlets blind for 10 minutes in the preheated oven, then carefully remove the paper and beans.

3 Melt the butter in a skillet and add the celery and leek and cook for 15 minutes, until soft. Add 2 tbsp heavy cream and crumble in the bleu cheese, mix well, and season with salt and pepper. Bring the remaining cream to a simmer in another pan, then pour onto the egg yolks, stirring all the time. Mix in the bleu cheese mixture and spoon into the pastry shells. Bake for 10 minutes, then turn the pan round in the oven and bake for an additional 5 minutes. Let cool in the pan for 5 minutes before serving.

SMOKED SALMON, DILL & HORSERADISH TARTLETS

MAKES 6
for the pie dough
heaping ¾ cup all-purpose flour, plus
    extra for dusting
pinch of salt
2½ oz/75 g cold butter, cut into pieces,
    plus extra for greasing
cold water

for the filling
½ cup sour cream
1 tsp creamed horseradish
½ tsp lemon juice
1 tsp Spanish capers, chopped
salt and pepper
3 egg yolks
7 oz/200 g smoked salmon trimmings
bunch fresh dill, chopped, plus extra
    sprigs to garnish

GRANDMA'S TIPS

*If you're short on time, you
can use store-bought pastry to
make the tartlets, or you can use
prepared tartlet cases instead. The
filling can also be used to make
one larger (8-inch/20-cm) tart
if you prefer—just increase the
baking time to 20–25 minutes.*

1 Grease six 3½-inch/9-cm loose-bottom fluted tart pans. Sift the flour and salt
into a food processor, add the butter, and process until the mixture resembles fine
breadcrumbs. Transfer the mixture to a large bowl and add a little cold water, just enough
to bring the dough together. Turn out onto a floured counter and divide into 6 equal-size
pieces. Roll each piece to fit the tart pans. Carefully fit each piece of dough in its shell
and press well to fit the pan. Roll the rolling pin over the pan to neaten the edges and
trim the excess dough. Cut 6 pieces of parchment paper and fit a piece into each tart, fill
with dried beans, and let chill in the refrigerator for 30 minutes. Meanwhile, preheat the
oven to 400°F/200°C.

2 Bake the tart shells blind for 10 minutes in the preheated oven, then remove the beans
and parchment paper.

3 Meanwhile, put the sour cream, horseradish, lemon juice, capers, and salt and pepper
into a bowl and mix well. Add the egg yolks, the smoked salmon, and the dill and
carefully mix again. Divide this mixture among the tart shells and return to the oven for
10 minutes. Let cool in the pans for 5 minutes before serving garnished with dill sprigs.

ROAST TURKEY
WITH STUFFING

SERVES 8
1 x 11-lb/5-kg turkey
4 tbsp butter
5 tbsp red wine
1¾ cups chicken stock
1 tbsp cornstarch
1 tsp French mustard
1 tsp sherry vinegar

for the stuffing
8 oz/225 g pork sausagemeat
8 oz/225 g unsweetened chestnut purée
3 oz/85 g walnuts
4 oz/115 g dried apricots, chopped
2 tbsp chopped fresh parsley
2 tbsp chopped fresh chives
2 tsp chopped fresh sage
4–5 tbsp heavy cream
salt and pepper

1 To make the stuffing, combine the sausagemeat and chestnut purée in a bowl, then stir in the walnuts, apricots, parsley, chives, and sage. Stir in enough cream to make a firm, but not dry, mixture. Season with salt and pepper.

2 Preheat the oven to 425°F/220°C. If you are planning to stuff the turkey, fill only the neck cavity and close the flap of skin with a skewer. Alternatively, the stuffing may be cooked separately, either rolled into small balls or spooned into an ovenproof dish, for the last 30–40 minutes of the cooking time.

3 Place the bird in a large roasting pan and rub all over with 3 tablespoons of the butter. Roast for 1 hour, then lower the oven temperature to 350°F/180°C and roast for an additional 2½ hours. You may need to pour off the fat from the roasting pan occasionally.

4 Check that the turkey is cooked by inserting a skewer or the point of a sharp knife into the thigh; if the juices run clear, it is ready. Transfer the bird to a carving board, cover loosely with foil, and let rest.

5 To make the gravy, skim off the fat from the roasting pan then place the pan over medium heat. Add the red wine and stir with a wooden spoon, scraping up the sediment from the bottom of the pan. Stir in the chicken stock. Mix the cornstarch, mustard, vinegar, and 2 teaspoons of water together in a small bowl, then stir into the wine and stock. Bring to a boil, stirring constantly until thickened and smooth. Stir in the remaining butter.

6 Carve the turkey and serve with the stuffing and gravy.

ROAST GOOSE WITH HONEY & PEARS

SERVES 4

1 oven-ready goose, weighing
   7 lb 12 oz–10 lb/3.5–4.5 kg
1 tsp salt
4 pears

1 tbsp lemon juice
4 tbsp butter
2 tbsp honey
seasonal vegetables, for serving

GRANDMA'S TIPS

While the goose is cooking, pour off the fat every 20 minutes and reserve. Strain and pour the fat into clean preserving jars. It will keep in the refrigerator for up to a year. Goose fat makes the best-ever roasted potatoes.

1 Preheat the oven to 425°F/220°C.

2 Rinse the goose and pat dry. Use a fork to prick the skin all over, then rub with the salt. Place the bird upside down on a rack in a roasting pan. Roast in the oven for 30 minutes. Drain off the fat. Turn the bird over and roast for 15 minutes. Drain off the fat. Reduce the temperature to 350°F/180°C and roast for 15 minutes per 1 lb/ 450 g. Cover with foil 15 minutes before the end of the cooking time. Check that the bird is cooked by inserting a knife between the legs and body. If the juices run clear, it is cooked. Remove from the oven.

3 Peel and halve the pears and brush with lemon juice. Melt the butter and honey in a pan over low heat, then add the pears. Cook, stirring, for 5–10 minutes until tender. Remove from the heat, arrange the pears around the goose, and pour the sweet juices over the bird. Serve with seasonal vegetables.

ROAST HAM

SERVES 8
1 × 9-lb/4-kg ham
1 apple, cored and chopped
1 onion, chopped
1 1/4 cups hard cider

6 black peppercorns
1 bouquet garni
1 bay leaf
about 50 cloves
4 tbsp raw brown sugar

GRANDMA'S TIPS

After removing the rind from the ham, try spreading 2 tablespoons of mustard over the fat to give the ham some extra flavor, then score the fat into a diamond-shaped pattern and stud with the cloves.

1 Put the ham in a large pan and add enough cold water to cover. Bring to a boil and skim off the foam that rises to the surface. Lower the heat and let simmer for 30 minutes. Drain the ham and return to the pan. Add the apple, onion, cider, peppercorns, bouquet garni, bay leaf, and a few of the cloves. Pour in enough fresh water to cover and return to a boil. Cover and let simmer for 3 hours 20 minutes.

2 Preheat the oven to 400°F/200°C. Take the pan off the heat and set aside to cool slightly. Remove the ham from the cooking liquid and, while it is still warm, loosen the rind with a sharp knife, then peel it off and discard. Score the fat into diamond shapes and stud with the remaining cloves. Place the ham on a rack in a roasting pan and sprinkle with the sugar. Roast, basting occasionally with the cooking liquid, for 20 minutes. Serve hot or cold.

FESTIVE BEEF
WELLINGTON

SERVES 4

1 lb 10 oz/750 g thick beef tenderloin
2 tbsp butter
salt and pepper
2 tbsp vegetable oil
1 garlic clove, chopped

1 onion, chopped
6 oz/175 g cremini mushrooms
1 tbsp chopped fresh sage
12 oz/350 g frozen puff pastry dough, thawed
1 egg, beaten

1 Preheat the oven to 425°F/220°C. Put the beef in a roasting pan, spread with butter, and season with salt and pepper. Roast for 30 minutes, then remove from the oven. Meanwhile, heat the oil in a pan over medium heat. Add the garlic and onion and cook, stirring, for 3 minutes. Stir in the mushrooms, sage, and salt and pepper to taste, and cook for 5 minutes. Remove from the heat.

2 Roll out the dough into a rectangle large enough to enclose the beef, then place the beef in the middle and spread the mushroom mixture over it. Bring the long sides of the dough together over the beef and seal with beaten egg. Tuck the short ends over (trim away excess dough) and seal. Place on a cookie sheet, seam-side down. Make 2 slits in the top. Decorate with dough shapes and brush with beaten egg. Bake for 40 minutes. If it browns too quickly, cover with foil. Remove from the oven, cut into thick slices, and serve hot.

RACK OF LAMB

SERVES 2
1 trimmed rack of lamb, weighing
   9–10½ oz/250–300 g
1 garlic clove, crushed
⅔ cup red wine
1 fresh rosemary sprig, crushed to
   release the flavor
salt and pepper
1 tbsp olive oil
⅔ cup lamb stock
2 tbsp red currant jelly

for the mint sauce
bunch fresh mint leaves
2 tsp superfine sugar
2 tbsp boiling water
2 tbsp white wine vinegar

GRANDMA'S TIPS

*This is an ideal roast to make
for just two people. For more,
double or triple the quantity.
It makes a very good dinner
party dish and is easy to carve.
Serve with a mixture of spring
vegetables and garnish with
rosemary.*

1 Place the rack of lamb in a nonmetallic bowl and rub all over with the garlic. Pour over the wine and place the rosemary sprig on top. Cover and let marinate in the refrigerator for 3 hours or overnight if possible.

2 Preheat the oven to 425°F/220°C. Remove the lamb from the marinade, reserving the marinade. Pat the meat dry with paper towels and season generously with salt and pepper. Place the lamb in a small roasting pan, drizzle with the oil, and roast for 15–20 minutes, depending on whether you like your meat pink or medium. Remove the lamb from the oven and let rest, covered with foil, in a warm place for 5 minutes.

3 Meanwhile, pour the reserved marinade into a small pan, bring to a boil over medium heat, and bubble gently for 2–3 minutes. Add the stock and red currant jelly and let simmer, stirring, until the mixture is syrupy.

4 To make the mint sauce, chop the fresh mint leaves and mix together with the sugar in a small bowl. Add the boiling water and stir to dissolve the sugar. Add the white wine vinegar and let stand for 30 minutes before serving with the lamb.

5 Carve the lamb into chops and serve on warmed plates with the sauce spooned over the top. Serve the mint sauce separately.

HERBED SALMON WITH HOLLANDAISE SAUCE

SERVES 4
4 salmon fillets, about 6 oz/175 g each, skin removed
salt and pepper
2 tbsp olive oil
1 tbsp chopped fresh dill
1 tbsp chopped fresh chives, plus extra for garnish

for the hollandaise sauce
3 egg yolks
1 tbsp water
salt and pepper
1 cup butter, cut into small cubes
juice of 1 lemon

for serving
freshly boiled new potatoes
freshly cooked broccoli
sesame seeds, for sprinkling (optional)

GRANDMA'S TIPS

Hollandaise is a difficult sauce to make, as it tends to separate. To simplify, boil the water with the lemon juice in a small pan. Place the egg yolks with the salt in a blender and blend. With the motor running, pour the lemon juice mixture over the egg yolks and blend. Melt the butter and add it to the blender in a steady stream until the mixture is thick. Hollandaise sauce should be served immediately after it has been made.

1 Preheat the broiler to medium. Rinse the fish fillets under cold running water and pat dry with paper towels. Season with salt and pepper. Combine the olive oil with the dill and chives, then brush the mixture over the fish. Transfer to the broiler and cook for about 6–8 minutes, turning once and brushing with more oil and herb mixture, until cooked to your taste.

2 Meanwhile, to make the hollandaise sauce, put the egg yolks in a heatproof bowl over a pan of boiling water. Add the water and season with salt and pepper. Lower the heat and simmer, whisking constantly, until the mixture begins to thicken. Whisk in the butter, cube by cube, until the mixture is thick and shiny. Whisk in the lemon juice, then remove from the heat.

3 Remove the fish from the broiler and transfer to individual serving plates. Pour over the sauce and garnish with chopped fresh chives. Serve with freshly boiled new potatoes and broccoli, and sprinkle with sesame seeds, if using.

MIXED NUT LOAF WITH CRANBERRY & RED WINE SAUCE

SERVES 4

2 tbsp butter, plus extra for greasing
2 garlic cloves, chopped
1 large onion, chopped
½ cup hazelnuts, toasted and ground
½ cup walnuts, ground
⅓ cup cashews, ground
½ cup pine nuts, toasted and ground
scant 2 cups whole wheat breadcrumbs
1 egg, lightly beaten

2 tbsp chopped fresh thyme
1 cup vegetable stock
salt and pepper
sprigs of fresh thyme, for garnish

for the cranberry & red wine sauce
1¾ cups fresh cranberries
½ cup superfine sugar
1¼ cups red wine
1 cinnamon stick

1 Preheat the oven to 350°F/180°C. Grease a loaf pan and line it with waxed paper. Melt the butter in a large pan over medium heat. Add the garlic and onion and cook, stirring, for 3 minutes, until softened. Remove from the heat and stir in the nuts, breadcrumbs, egg, thyme, and stock. Season to taste with salt and pepper.

2 Spoon the mixture into the loaf pan and level the surface. Cook in the center of the preheated oven for 30 minutes or until cooked through and golden brown. The loaf is done when a skewer inserted into the center comes out clean. About halfway through the cooking time, make the cranberry and red wine sauce. Put all the ingredients into a pan and bring to a boil. Reduce the heat and simmer, stirring occasionally, for 15 minutes.

3 For serving, remove the sauce from the heat and discard the cinnamon stick. Remove the nut loaf from the oven and turn out. Garnish with sprigs of thyme and serve with the cranberry and red wine sauce.

ROASTED POTATOES

SERVES 6
3 lb/1.3 kg large potatoes, such as round white, round red, or fingerling, peeled and cut into even-size chunks

salt
3 tbsp goose fat, duck fat, or olive oil

GRANDMA'S TIPS

The potatoes can be seasoned while they're roasting, which allows the flavors to be absorbed. Parsnips can be roasted in the same way but they'll only need 2–3 minutes precooking and they don't need to be shaken in the pan.

1 Preheat the oven to 425°F/220°C.

2 Cook the potatoes in a large pan of lightly salted boiling water over medium heat, covered, for 5–7 minutes. They will still be firm. Remove from the heat. Meanwhile, add the fat to a roasting pan and place in the hot oven.

3 Drain the potatoes well and return them to the pan. Cover with the lid and firmly shake the pan so that the surface of the potatoes is slightly roughened to help give them a much crisper texture.

4 Remove the roasting pan from the oven and carefully turn the potatoes into the hot fat. Baste them to ensure that they are all coated with it.

5 Roast the potatoes at the top of the oven for 45–50 minutes until they are browned all over and thoroughly crisp. Turn the potatoes and baste again only once during the process or the crunchy edges will be destroyed.

6 Using a slotted spoon, carefully transfer the potatoes from the roasting pan into a warmed serving dish. Sprinkle with a little salt and serve at once. Any leftovers (although this is most unlikely) are delicious cold.

CANDIED SWEET POTATOES

SWEET

SERVES 4–6

3 large orange-fleshed sweet potatoes, about 9 oz/250 g each, scrubbed
2 tbsp butter, melted and cooled, plus extra for greasing

¼ cup brown sugar
finely grated rind of ½ orange
4 tbsp freshly squeezed orange juice
pinch of cayenne pepper, or to taste (optional)

GRANDMA'S TIPS

Candied root vegetables are all delicious—try parsnips, carrots, and baby turnips. Go easy on the sugar as they all contain their own natural sweetness.

1 Bring a large pan of water to a boil over high heat. Add the sweet potatoes and cook for 15 minutes. Drain, then put them under cold running water to cool. When cool enough to handle, peel, then cut each into 8 wedges or chunks.

2 Preheat the oven to 400°F/200°C. Lightly grease a baking dish large enough to hold all the wedges or chunks in a single layer, and add the partially cooked potatoes.

3 Put the butter, sugar, and orange rind and juice into a small pan over medium heat and stir until the sugar dissolves. Bring to a boil and boil until the liquid reduces by about one-third. Stir in the cayenne pepper, if using.

4 Generously brush the sweet potatoes with the glaze. Bake in the oven, glazing an additional 2–3 times at intervals, for 20–30 minutes until the sweet potatoes are tender when pierced with the tip of a knife or a skewer. These are excellent served hot, but are also delicious if left to cool and served as part of a picnic or barbecue spread.

ROASTED ROOT VEGETABLES

SERVES 4–6

3 parsnips, cut into 2-inch/5-cm chunks
4 baby turnips, quartered
3 carrots, cut into 2-inch/5-cm chunks
1 lb/450 g butternut squash, peeled and
  cut into 2-inch/5-cm chunks
1 lb/450 g sweet potatoes, peeled and
  cut into 2-inch/5-cm chunks
2 garlic cloves, finely chopped
2 tbsp chopped fresh rosemary
2 tbsp chopped fresh thyme
2 tsp chopped fresh sage
3 tbsp olive oil
salt and pepper
2 tbsp chopped fresh mixed herbs, such
  as parsley, thyme, and mint, for garnish

1 Preheat the oven to 425°F/220°C.

2 Arrange all the vegetables in a single layer in a large roasting pan. Sprinkle over the garlic and the herbs. Pour over the oil and season well with salt and pepper.

3 Toss all the ingredients together until they are well mixed and coated with the oil (you can let them marinate at this stage to allow the flavors to be absorbed).

4 Roast the vegetables at the top of the oven for 50–60 minutes until they are cooked and nicely browned. Turn the vegetables over halfway through the cooking time.

5 Serve with a good handful of fresh herbs sprinkled on top and a final seasoning of salt and pepper to taste.

HONEYED PARSNIPS

SERVES 4
8 parsnips, peeled and cut into quarters
4 tbsp vegetable oil
1 tbsp honey

GRANDMA'S TIPS

For a change try substituting maple syrup for the honey or use a mixture of root vegetables for a colorful dish.

1 Preheat the oven to 350°F/180°C.

2 Bring a large pan of water to a boil. Reduce the heat, add the parsnips, and cook for 5 minutes. Drain thoroughly.

3 Pour 2 tablespoons of the oil into a shallow, ovenproof dish and add the parsnips. Mix the remaining oil with the honey and drizzle over the parsnips. Roast in the preheated oven for 45 minutes until golden brown and tender. Remove from the oven and serve.

BRUSSELS SPROUTS WITH BUTTERED CHESTNUTS

SERVES 4
12 oz/350 g Brussels sprouts, trimmed
3 tbsp butter
3½ oz/100 g canned whole chestnuts

pinch of nutmeg
salt and pepper
½ cup slivered almonds, for garnish

GRANDMA'S TIPS

Take care when buying canned chestnuts not to buy the sweetened ones. Instead of canned chestnuts, try the vacuum-packed ones, which are easy to find and use. Dried chestnuts are available from natural foods stores but they'll need a good soaking, preferably overnight, before using.

1 Bring a large pan of water to a boil. Add the Brussels sprouts and cook for 5 minutes. Drain thoroughly.

2 Melt the butter in a large pan over medium heat. Add the Brussels sprouts and cook, stirring, for 3 minutes, then add the chestnuts and nutmeg. Season with salt and pepper and stir well. Cook for another 2 minutes, stirring, then remove from the heat. Transfer to a serving dish, scatter over the almonds, and serve.

HONEY-GLAZED RED CABBAGE WITH GOLDEN RAISINS

SERVES 4

2 tbsp butter
1 garlic clove, chopped
1 lb 7 oz/650 g red cabbage, shredded

scant 1 cup golden raisins
1 tbsp honey
scant ½ cup red wine
scant ½ cup water

1 Melt the butter in a large pan over medium heat. Add the garlic and cook, stirring, for 1 minute, until slightly softened.

2 Add the cabbage and golden raisins, then stir in the honey. Cook for another minute. Pour in the wine and water and bring to a boil. Reduce the heat, cover, and simmer, stirring occasionally, for about 45 minutes, or until the cabbage is cooked. Serve hot.

PUMPKIN PIE

SERVES 6

4 lb/1.8 kg pumpkin
4 tbsp cold unsalted butter, in small pieces, plus extra for greasing
1 cup all-purpose flour, plus extra for dusting
¼ tsp baking powder
1½ tsp ground cinnamon
¾ tsp ground nutmeg
¾ tsp ground cloves
1 tsp salt
¼ cup superfine sugar
3 eggs

1¾ cups sweetened condensed milk
½ tsp vanilla extract
1 tbsp raw sugar

for the streusel topping
2 tbsp all-purpose flour
4 tbsp raw brown sugar
1 tsp ground cinnamon
2 tbsp cold unsalted butter, in small pieces
heaping ⅔ cup shelled pecans, chopped
heaping ⅔ cup shelled walnuts, chopped

GRANDMA'S TIPS

Luckily we can use prepared pie pastry and cans of pumpkin purée, which reduce the time needed to make this traditional Thanksgiving dish (particularly when we have so much else to prepare for the big day). The streusel topping can also be made quickly with the help of a food processor.

1 Preheat the oven to 375°F/190°C. Halve the pumpkin, remove the seeds, and set aside for roasting. Remove and discard the stem and stringy insides. Place the pumpkin halves, face down, in a shallow baking pan and cover with foil. Bake in the preheated oven for 1½ hours, then remove from the oven and let cool. Scoop out the flesh and mash with a potato masher or purée it in a food processor. Drain away any excess liquid. Cover with plastic wrap and let chill until ready to use. It will keep for 3 days (or several months in a freezer).

2 Grease a 9-inch/23-cm round pie dish with butter. To make the pie dough, sift the flour and baking powder into a large bowl. Stir in ½ tsp cinnamon, ¼ tsp nutmeg, ¼ tsp cloves, ½ tsp salt, and all the superfine sugar. Rub in the butter with your fingertips until the mixture resembles fine breadcrumbs, then make a well in the center. Lightly beat 1 egg and pour it into the well. Mix together with a wooden spoon, then use your hands to shape the dough into a ball. Place it on a clean counter lightly dusted with flour, and roll out to a circle large enough to line the pie dish. Use it to line the dish, then trim the edges. Cover the dish with plastic wrap and let chill in the refrigerator for 30 minutes.

3 Preheat the oven to 425°F/220°C. To make the filling, place the pumpkin purée in a large bowl, then stir in the condensed milk and remaining eggs. Add the remaining spices and salt, then stir in the vanilla extract and raw sugar. Pour into the pastry shell and bake for 15 minutes.

4 Meanwhile, make the streusel topping. Combine the flour, sugar, and cinnamon in a bowl, rub in the butter until crumbly, then stir in the nuts. Remove the pie from the oven and reduce the heat to 350°F/180°C. Sprinkle the topping over the pie, then bake for an additional 35 minutes. Remove from the oven and serve hot or cold.

CLASSIC PUMPKIN PIE
RECIPE ON REVERSE
VISIT WWW.CARNATIONMILK.CA

QUALITY MILK

Carnation®

Excellent Source Of Protein

VITAMINS C & D Added

Evaporated Milk

MILK, DISODIUM
E (VITAMIN C),
OL (VITAMIN D),
RE, PHOSPHATE
UM (VITAMINE C),
OL (VITAMINE D),

TORE IN A COOL,
NCE OPENING.

S SEC, BIEN AGITER
ÈS OUVERTURE.
DE CAN, MEILLEURE SI
DESSOUS DE LA BOÎTE.

SIT:
USES
SITER :
ILK.CA

3451

370

00308 5

PECAN PIE

SERVES 8

for the pie dough
heaping 1 ½ cups all-purpose flour
pinch of salt
½ cup butter, cut into small pieces
1 tbsp lard or vegetable shortening, cut
  into small pieces
heaping ¼ cup superfine sugar
6 tbsp cold milk

whipped cream or vanilla ice cream,
  for serving

for the filling
3 eggs
heaping 1 cup dark brown sugar
1 tsp vanilla extract
pinch of salt
6 tbsp butter, melted
3 tbsp corn syrup
3 tbsp molasses
2 cups shelled pecans, roughly chopped
pecan halves, for decorating

GRANDMA'S TIPS

To bake the pastry blind you don't have to use dried beans—instead buy some ceramic "beans," which are heavier and can be used indefinitely. Lining the pastry with foil will help conduct the heat more evenly.

1 To make the pie dough, sift the flour and salt into a mixing bowl and rub in the butter and lard with your fingertips until the mixture resembles fine breadcrumbs. Work in the superfine sugar and add the milk. Work the mixture into a soft dough. Wrap the dough and let chill in the refrigerator for 30 minutes.

2 Preheat the oven to 400°F/200°C. Roll out the pie dough and use it to line a 9–10-inch/23–25-cm tart pan. Trim off the excess by running the rolling pin over the top of the tart pan. Line with parchment paper, and fill with dried beans. Bake in the oven for 20 minutes. Take out of the oven and remove the paper and dried beans. Reduce the oven temperature to 350°F/180°C. Place a cookie sheet in the oven.

3 To make the filling, place the eggs in a bowl and beat lightly. Beat in the dark brown sugar, vanilla extract, and salt. Stir in the butter, corn syrup, molasses, and chopped nuts. Pour into the pastry shell and decorate with the pecan halves.

4 Place on the heated cookie sheet and bake in the oven for 35–40 minutes until the filling is set. Serve warm or at room temperature with whipped cream or vanilla ice cream.

CHRISTMAS COOKIES

MAKES 24
½ cup superfine sugar
1 cup butter, plus extra for greasing
3 cups all-purpose flour, plus extra
    for dusting
pinch of salt

for decorating
½ cup confectioners' sugar
edible cake decorations, such as silver
    balls

1 Beat the sugar and butter together in a large bowl until combined (thorough creaming is not necessary).

2 Sift in the flour and salt and work together to form a stiff dough. Turn out on to a lightly floured surface. Knead lightly for a few moments until smooth, but avoid overhandling. Chill in the refrigerator for 10–15 minutes.

3 Preheat the oven to 350°F/180°C. Roll out the dough on a lightly floured work surface and cut into shapes with small Christmas cutters, such as holly leaves, stars, and Christmas trees. Place on greased cookie sheets.

4 Bake the cookies in the preheated oven for 10–15 minutes, until pale golden brown. Leave on the cookie sheets for 10 minutes, then transfer to wire racks to cool completely.

5 Mix the confectioners' sugar with a little water to make a frosting, and use to frost the cookies. Decorate with silver balls or other edible cake decorations. Store in an airtight container or wrap the cookies individually in cellophane, tie with colored ribbon or string, and then hang them on the Christmas tree as edible decorations.

SPICED PUNCH

SERVES 10
4 cups red wine
4 tbsp sugar
1 cinnamon stick
1 ¾ cups boiling water
scant ½ cup brandy
scant ½ cup sherry

scant ½ cup orange liqueur, such as
   Cointreau
2 seedless oranges, cut into wedges
2 dessert apples, cored and cut into
   wedges

GRANDMA'S TIPS

You should use heatproof glasses to serve this hot punch. If you are concerned that your glasses may be too fragile, place a metal teaspoon in each glass as you pour so that some of the heat is absorbed by the metal.

1 Put the wine, sugar, and cinnamon into a large pan and stir together well. Warm over low heat, stirring, until just starting to simmer, but do not let it boil. Remove from the heat and pour through a strainer. Discard the cinnamon stick.

2 Return the wine to the pan and stir in the water, brandy, sherry, and orange liqueur. Add the orange and apple wedges and warm gently over very low heat, but do not let it boil. Remove from the heat and pour into a large, heatproof punch bowl. Ladle into heatproof glasses and serve hot.

Those with a sweet tooth will fondly remember the delicious aromas of the desserts that would emanate from Grandma's kitchen. Some are really quick and easy to assemble, while others take more time, making them best reserved for special occasions and family get-togethers. Chocolate mousse is always popular, and, together with Mississippi mud pie and Black Forest cake, will give even the biggest chocoholic enough recipes to indulge in. Apple and cherry pies and a peach cobbler are included to add fruit to the menu—the

GRANDMA'S JUST DESSERTS

fruit can be changed according to taste and season, providing even more diversity. Along with traditional favorites, such as cheesecake, baked apples, and good old rice pudding, you will find recipes for more exotic—but equally well-loved—desserts like Italian tiramisù and profiteroles. These are dishes that we've grown up with and adopted as our own, despite their far-flung origins. With such a wide selection you'll certainly have your pick of recipes when it comes to choosing your Grandma's favorite desserts.

APPLE PIE

SERVES 6
for the pie dough
2½ cups all-purpose flour
pinch of salt
6 tbsp butter or margarine, cut into
  small pieces
6 tbsp lard or vegetable shortening, cut
  into small pieces
about 6 tbsp cold water
beaten egg or milk, for glazing

for the filling
1 lb 10 oz–2 lb 4 oz/750 g–1 kg baking
  apples, peeled, cored, and sliced
scant ⅔ cup superfine sugar, plus extra
  for sprinkling
½–1 tsp ground cinnamon, allspice,
  or ground ginger
1–2 tbsp water (optional)

GRANDMA'S TIPS

When preparing your apples make sure you get them ready one at a time, rather than peeling them all and then slicing them. As you go along, place the apple slices in a bowl of water with the juice of 1 lemon—this will stop them from discoloring.

1 To make the pie dough, sift the flour and salt into a large bowl. Add the butter and lard and rub in with your fingertips until the mixture resembles fine breadcrumbs. Add the water and gather the mixture together into a dough. Wrap the dough and let chill in the refrigerator for 30 minutes.

2 Preheat the oven to 425°F/220°C. Roll out almost two-thirds of the pie dough thinly and use to line a deep 9-inch/23-cm pie plate or pie pan.

3 Mix the apples with the sugar and spice and pack into the pastry shell; the filling can come up above the rim. Add the water if needed, particularly if the apples are a dry variety.

4 Roll out the remaining pie dough to form a lid. Dampen the edges of the pie rim with water and position the lid, pressing the edges firmly together. Trim and crimp the edges.

5 Use the trimmings to cut out leaves or other shapes to decorate the top of the pie, dampen and attach. Glaze the top of the pie with beaten egg or milk, make 1–2 slits in the top, and place the pie on a cookie sheet.

6 Bake in the preheated oven for 20 minutes, then reduce the temperature to 350°F/180°C and bake for an additional 30 minutes, or until the pastry is a light golden brown. Serve hot or cold, sprinkled with sugar.

LATTICED CHERRY PIE

SERVES 8

for the pie dough
1 cup all-purpose flour, plus extra
   for dusting
¼ tsp baking powder
½ tsp allspice
½ tsp salt
¼ cup sugar
6 tbsp cold unsalted butter, diced, plus
   extra for greasing
1 beaten egg, plus extra for glazing
water, for sealing

for the filling
2 lb/900 g pitted fresh or canned
   cherries, drained
¾ cup sugar
½ tsp almond extract
2 tsp cherry brandy
¼ tsp allspice
2 tbsp cornstarch
2 tbsp water

freshly whipped cream or ice cream,
   for serving

GRANDMA'S TIPS

This pie can be made using other fruits, such as blackberries. To complement the blackberries, substitute 2 teaspoons of cassis liqueur for the cherry brandy.

1 To make the pie dough, sift the flour and baking powder into a large bowl. Stir in the allspice, salt, and sugar. Using your fingertips, rub in 4 tablespoons of butter until the mixture resembles fine breadcrumbs, then make a well in the center. Pour the beaten egg into the well. Mix with a wooden spoon, then shape the mixture into a dough. Cut the dough in half and use your hands to roll each half into a ball. Wrap the dough and let chill in the refrigerator for 30 minutes.

2 Preheat the oven to 425°F/220°C. Grease a 9-inch/23-cm round pie dish with butter. Roll out the dough into 2 circles, each 12 inches/30 cm in diameter. Use one to line the pie dish. Trim the edges, leaving an overhang of ½ inch/1 cm.

3 To make the filling, place half the cherries and all the sugar in a large pan. Bring to a simmer over low heat, stirring, for 5 minutes, or until the sugar has melted. Stir in the almond extract, brandy, and allspice. In a separate bowl, mix the cornstarch and water to form a paste. Remove the pan from the heat, stir in the cornstarch, then return to the heat and stir constantly until the mixture boils and thickens. Let cool a little. Stir in the remaining cherries, pour into the pastry shell, then dot with the remaining butter.

4 Cut the dough circle into long strips ½ inch/1 cm wide. Lay 5 strips evenly across the top of the filling in the same direction, folding back every other strip. Now lay 6 strips crosswise over the strips, folding back every other strip each time you add another crosswise strip, to form a lattice. Trim off the ends and seal the edges with water. Use your fingers to crimp around the rim, then brush the top with beaten egg. Cover with foil, then bake for 30 minutes. Remove from the oven, discard the foil, then return the pie to the oven for an additional 15 minutes, or until cooked and golden. Serve warm with freshly whipped cream or ice cream.

PEAR & PECAN STRUDEL

SERVES 4

2 ripe pears
4 tbsp butter
1 cup fresh white breadcrumbs
heaping ⅓ cup shelled pecans, chopped
heaping ⅛ cup light brown sugar
finely grated rind of 1 orange

3½ oz/100 g filo pastry, thawed
  if frozen
6 tbsp orange blossom honey
2 tbsp orange juice
sifted confectioners' sugar, for dusting
strained plain yogurt, for serving
  (optional)

1 Preheat the oven to 400°F/200°C. Peel, core, and chop the pears. Melt 1 tablespoon of the butter in a skillet and gently sauté the breadcrumbs until golden. Transfer the breadcrumbs to a bowl and add the pears, nuts, light brown sugar, and orange rind. Place the remaining butter in a small pan and heat until melted.

2 Set aside 1 sheet of filo pastry, keeping it well wrapped, and brush the remaining filo sheets with a little melted butter. Spoon some of the nut filling onto the first filo sheet, leaving a 1-inch/2.5-cm margin around the edge. Build up the strudel by placing more buttered filo sheets on top of the first, spreading each one with nut filling as you build up the layers. Drizzle the honey and orange juice over the top.

3 Fold the short ends over the filling, then roll up, starting at a long side. Carefully lift onto a baking sheet, with the seam facing up. Brush with any remaining melted butter and crumple the reserved sheet of filo pastry around the strudel. Bake for 25 minutes, or until golden and crisp. Dust with sifted confectioners' sugar and serve warm with strained plain yogurt, if using.

PEACH COBBLER

SERVES 4–6
for the filling
6 peaches, peeled and sliced
4 tbsp superfine sugar
½ tbsp lemon juice
1½ tsp cornstarch
½ tsp almond or vanilla extract

vanilla or butter pecan ice cream,
  for serving

for the pie topping
scant 1¼ cups all-purpose flour
heaping ½ cup superfine sugar
1½ tsp baking powder
½ tsp salt
6 tbsp butter, diced
1 egg
5–6 tbsp milk

GRANDMA'S TIPS
*The peaches can be replaced
with apricots when they are in
season—you will need two to
three times the amount and they
don't need to be peeled. You can
use canned fruit (which doesn't
need cooking) and thicken the
juice with the cornstarch before
spooning the filling into the dish.*

1 Preheat the oven to 425°F/220°C. Place the peaches in a 9-inch/23-cm square ovenproof dish that is also suitable for serving. Add the sugar, lemon juice, cornstarch, and almond extract and toss together. Bake the peaches in the oven for 20 minutes.

2 Meanwhile, to make the topping, sift the flour, all but 2 tablespoons of the sugar, the baking powder, and salt into a bowl. Rub in the butter with your fingertips until the mixture resembles breadcrumbs. Mix the egg and 5 tablespoons of the milk in a pitcher, then mix into the dry ingredients with a fork until a soft, sticky dough forms. If the dough seems too dry, stir in the extra tablespoon of milk.

3 Reduce the oven temperature to 400°F/200°C. Remove the peaches from the oven and drop spoonfuls of the topping over the surface, without smoothing. Sprinkle with the remaining sugar, return to the oven, and bake for an additional 15 minutes, or until the topping is golden brown and firm—the topping will spread as it cooks. Serve hot or at room temperature with ice cream.

LEMON MERINGUE PIE

SERVES 4
for the pie dough
heaping 1 cup all-purpose flour, plus
    extra for dusting
6 tbsp butter, cut into small pieces, plus
    extra for greasing
¼ cup confectioners' sugar, sifted
finely grated rind of ½ lemon
½ egg yolk, beaten
1 ½ tbsp milk

for the filling
3 tbsp cornstarch
1 ¼ cups water
juice and grated rind of 2 lemons
heaping ¾ cup superfine sugar
2 eggs, separated

GRANDMA'S TIPS

*This pie is usually served cold,
but why not try it hot? It may
sound rather decadent but hot
lemon meringue pie with cold
ice cream is to die for. For a
change, limes or oranges can be
substituted for the lemons.*

1 To make the pie dough, sift the flour into a bowl. Rub in the butter with your
fingertips until the mixture resembles fine breadcrumbs. Mix in the remaining
ingredients. Knead briefly on a lightly floured counter. Let rest for 30 minutes.

2 Preheat the oven to 350°F/180°C. Grease an 8-inch/20-cm pie dish with butter. Roll
out the pie dough to a thickness of ¼ inch/5 mm; use it to line the base and sides of the
dish. Prick all over with a fork, line with parchment paper and fill with dried beans. Bake
in the oven for 15 minutes. Remove from the oven and take out the paper and beans.
Reduce the temperature to 300°F/150°C.

3 To make the filling, mix the cornstarch with a little of the water. Place the remaining
water in a pan. Stir in the lemon juice and rind and cornstarch paste. Bring to a boil,
stirring.

4 Cook for 2 minutes. Let cool a little. Stir in 5 tablespoons of the sugar and the egg
yolks and pour into the pastry shell.

5 Whisk the egg whites in a clean, greasefree bowl until stiff. Whisk in the remaining
sugar and spread over the pie. Bake for another 40 minutes. Remove from the oven, cool,
and serve.

MISSISSIPPI MUD PIE

SERVES 8

for the pie dough
1½ cups all-purpose flour, plus extra
   for dusting
2 tbsp unsweetened cocoa
½ cup butter
2 tbsp superfine sugar
1–2 tbsp cold water

for the filling
¾ cup butter
scant 1¾ cups dark brown sugar

4 eggs, lightly beaten
4 tbsp unsweetened cocoa, sifted
5½ oz/150 g semisweet chocolate
1¼ cups light cream
1 tsp chocolate extract

for decorating
scant 2 cups heavy cream, whipped
chocolate flakes and curls

1 To make the pie dough, sift the flour and cocoa into a mixing bowl. Rub in the butter with your fingertips until the mixture resembles fine breadcrumbs. Stir in the sugar and enough cold water to mix to a soft dough. Wrap the dough and let chill in the refrigerator for 15 minutes.

2 Preheat the oven to 375°F/190°C. Roll out the dough on a lightly floured counter and use to line a 9-inch/23-cm loose-bottom tart pan or ceramic pie dish. Line with parchment paper and fill with dried beans. Bake in the oven for 15 minutes. Remove from the oven and take out the paper and beans. Bake the pastry shell for an additional 10 minutes.

3 To make the filling, beat the butter and sugar together in a bowl and gradually beat in the eggs with the cocoa. Melt the chocolate and beat it into the mixture with the light cream and the chocolate extract.

4 Reduce the oven temperature to 325°F/160°C. Pour the mixture into the pastry shell and bake for 45 minutes, or until the filling has set gently.

5 Let the mud pie cool completely, then transfer it to a serving plate, if you like. Cover with the whipped cream.

6 Decorate the pie with chocolate flakes and curls and then let chill until ready to serve.

KEY LIME PIE

SERVES 8
for the crumb crust
6 oz/175 g graham crackers or
  gingersnaps
2 tbsp superfine sugar
½ tsp ground cinnamon
5 tbsp butter, melted

for the filling
butter, for greasing
1 ¾ cups canned sweetened condensed
  milk
½ cup freshly squeezed lime juice
finely grated rind of 3 limes, plus extra
  for decorating
4 egg yolks
whipped cream, for serving

GRANDMA'S TIPS
Key limes are smaller and more acidic than the more common Persian lime, but they are not widely available commercially. It is fine to use regular limes in this recipe. The crumb crust is traditional, but to save time you can use a prepared pie shell.

1 Preheat the oven to 325°F/160°C. Lightly grease a 9-inch/23-cm pie plate, about 1½ inches/4 cm deep.

2 To make the crumb crust, place the graham crackers, sugar, and cinnamon in a food processor and process until fine crumbs form—do not overprocess to a powder. Add the melted butter and process again until moistened.

3 Turn the crumb mixture into the pie plate and press over the base and up the sides. Place the pie plate on a cookie sheet and bake in the oven for 5 minutes.

4 Meanwhile, beat the condensed milk, lime juice, lime rind, and egg yolks together in a bowl until well blended.

5 Remove the crumb crust from the oven, pour the filling into the crumb crust, and spread out to the edges. Return to the oven for an additional 15 minutes, or until the filling is set around the edges but still wobbly in the center.

6 Let cool completely on a wire rack, then cover and let chill for at least 2 hours. Serve spread thickly with the whipped cream and decorated with grated lime rind.

SWEET POTATO PIE

SERVES 8

for the pie dough
scant 1 ¼ cups all-purpose flour, plus extra for dusting
½ tsp salt
¼ tsp superfine sugar
3 ½ tbsp butter, cut into small pieces
3 tbsp vegetable shortening, cut into small pieces
2–2 ½ tbsp cold water

whipped cream, for serving

for the filling
1 lb 2 oz/500 g orange-fleshed sweet potatoes
3 eggs, beaten
½ cup light brown sugar
1 ½ cups canned evaporated milk
3 tbsp butter, melted
2 tsp vanilla extract
1 tsp ground cinnamon
1 tsp ground nutmeg or freshly grated nutmeg
½ tsp salt

GRANDMA'S TIPS

This pie can be made using an equal amount of pumpkin or winter squash flesh. For a more elaborate presentation, pipe the cream around the edges of the pie.

1 To make the pie dough, sift the flour, salt, and sugar into a bowl. Add the butter and vegetable shortening and rub in with your fingertips until the mixture resembles fine breadcrumbs. Sprinkle over 2 tablespoons of the water and mix with a fork to make a soft dough. If the pie dough is too dry, sprinkle in an extra ½ tablespoon of water. Wrap the dough and let chill in the refrigerator for at least 1 hour.

2 Meanwhile, bring a large pan of water to a boil over high heat. Peel and add the sweet potatoes and cook for 15 minutes. Drain, then cool them under cold running water. When cool, cut each into 8 wedges. Put the sweet potatoes in a separate bowl and beat in the eggs and brown sugar until very smooth. Beat in the remaining ingredients, then set aside until ready to use.

3 When ready to bake, preheat the oven to 425°F/220°C. Roll out the pie dough on a lightly floured counter into a thin 11-inch/28-cm circle and use to line a deep 9-inch/23-cm pie plate or pie pan (about 1¼ inches/4 cm deep). Trim off the excess pie dough and press the floured fork around the edges.

4 Prick the base of the pastry shell all over with the fork. Line with parchment paper and fill with dried beans. Bake in the oven for 12 minutes until lightly golden.

5 Remove the pastry shell from the oven and take out the paper and beans. Pour the filling into the pastry shell, and return to the oven for an additional 10 minutes. Reduce the oven temperature to 325°F/160°C and bake for an additional 35 minutes. Let cool on a wire rack. Serve warm or at room temperature with whipped cream.

NEW YORK CHEESECAKE WITH BLUEBERRY COMPOTE

SERVES 8–10
canola oil, for brushing
6 tbsp unsalted butter
7 oz/200 g graham crackers, crushed
1 lb/450 g full-fat cream cheese
7 tbsp superfine sugar
2 large eggs
1 large egg yolk
7 tbsp sour cream
1 ½ tsp vanilla extract

for the topping
1 ¾ cups sour cream
¼ cup superfine sugar

for the blueberry compote
¼ cup superfine sugar
4 tbsp water
1 cup fresh blueberries
1 tsp arrowroot

1 Preheat the oven to 300°F/150°C. Brush a 20-cm/8-inch springform cake pan with oil. Melt the butter in a saucepan over low heat. Stir in the graham crackers and press evenly into the base of the pan. Bake for 10 minutes, or until lightly browned, then remove and set aside to cool.

2 Place the cream cheese into a large bowl and beat until smooth. Add the sugar and beat for 1 minute. Add the eggs and egg yolk and beat until well combined. Add the sour cream and vanilla extract and stir until smooth. Pour the mixture into the pan and spread evenly.

3 Bake in the oven for 35–45 minutes or until the edges are firm but the center is still slightly soft.

4 Remove from the oven and place on a wire rack (still in the pan). Increase the oven temperature to 400°F/200°C.

5 To make the topping, mix together the sour cream and superfine sugar, and spread over the top of the cheesecake. Place in the oven and bake for 5–7 minutes until the topping has become very liquid. Turn the oven off but leave the cheesecake inside for 1 hour. Remove from the oven and cool in the pan on a wire rack. Cover and refrigerate overnight.

6 To make the compote, combine the sugar and half the water in a small saucepan and stir over low heat until the sugar has dissolved. Increase the heat, add the blueberries, then cover and cook for 2–3 minutes or until the blueberries begin to soften. Remove from the heat. Stir together the arrowroot and remaining water in a cup to dissolve the arrowroot. Add to the fruit, return to low heat, and stir until the juice thickens and turns translucent. Leave to cool completely.

7 Remove the cheesecake from the pan 30 minutes before serving. Spoon the fruit on top and chill until ready to serve.

BLACK FOREST CAKE

SERVES 8

3 tbsp unsalted butter, melted, plus extra
  for greasing
2 lb/900 g fresh cherries, pitted and
  halved
1 1/4 cups superfine sugar
scant 1/2 cup cherry brandy
3/4 cup all-purpose flour

5 tbsp cocoa powder
1/2 tsp baking powder
4 eggs
4 cups heavy cream

for decorating
grated dark chocolate
whole fresh cherries

GRANDMA'S TIPS

*It's possible to make this
extravagant cake using canned
cherries—drain the fruit from
the juice and use the liquid to
soak the cake before assembling.
Kirsch or brandy can be used
instead of the cherry brandy.*

1 Preheat the oven to 350°F/180°C. Grease and line a 9-inch/23-cm springform cake
pan. Place the cherries in a saucepan, add 3 tablespoons of the sugar and the cherry
brandy and bring to a simmer over medium heat. Simmer for 5 minutes. Drain, reserving
the syrup. In a large bowl, sift together the flour, cocoa, and baking powder.

2 Place the eggs in a heatproof bowl and beat in 3/4 cup of the sugar. Place the bowl
over a saucepan of simmering water and beat for 6 minutes, or until thickened. Remove
from the heat, then gradually fold in the flour mixture and melted butter. Spoon into the
cake pan and bake for 40 minutes. Remove from the oven and leave to cool in the pan.

3 Turn out the cake and cut in half horizontally. Mix the heavy cream and the remaining
sugar together and whip lightly until soft peaks form. Spread the reserved syrup over
the cut sides of the cake, then top with a layer of whipped cream. Arrange the cherries
over half of the cake, then place the other half on top. Cover the top of the cake with
whipped cream, sprinkle over the grated chocolate, and decorate with the whole fresh
cherries.

PROFITEROLES

SERVES 4
for the choux pastry
5 tbsp butter, plus extra for greasing
¾ cup cold water
¾ cup all-purpose flour
3 eggs, beaten

for the cream filling
1¼ cups heavy cream
3 tbsp superfine sugar
1 tsp vanilla extract

for the chocolate & brandy sauce
4½ oz/125 g semisweet chocolate,
   broken into pieces
2½ tbsp butter
6 tbsp water
2 tbsp brandy

GRANDMA'S TIPS

*The choux puffs can be made
two to three days ahead and kept
in an airtight container until
needed. The empty puffs can also
be filled with savory mixtures,
like shrimp and mayonnaise, to
serve with drinks.*

1 Preheat the oven to 400°F/200°C.

2 Grease a large cookie sheet with butter. To make the pastry, place the water and butter in a pan and bring to a boil. Meanwhile, sift the flour into a bowl. Remove the pan from the heat and beat in the flour until smooth. Cool for 5 minutes. Beat in enough of the eggs to give the mixture a soft, dropping consistency. Transfer to a piping bag fitted with a ¹/2-inch/1-cm plain tip. Pipe small balls onto the cookie sheet. Bake for 25 minutes. Remove from the oven. Pierce each ball with a skewer to let steam escape.

3 To make the filling, whip together the cream, sugar, and vanilla extract. Cut the pastry balls almost in half, then fill with the cream filling.

4 To make the sauce, gently melt the chocolate and butter with the water in a small saucepan, stirring, until smooth. Stir in the brandy. Pile the profiteroles into individual serving dishes or into a pyramid on a raised cake stand. Pour over the sauce and serve.

CHOCOLATE MOUSSE

SERVES 4
10½ oz/300 g semisweet chocolate
1½ tbsp unsalted butter
1 tbsp brandy
4 eggs, separated
cocoa powder, for dusting

1 Break the chocolate into small pieces and place in a heatproof bowl set over a pan of simmering water. Add the butter and melt with the chocolate, stirring, until smooth. Remove from the heat, stir in the brandy and let cool slightly. Add the egg yolks and beat until smooth.

2 In a separate bowl, whisk the egg whites until stiff peaks have formed, then fold them into the chocolate mixture. Spoon the mixture into 4 small serving bowls and level the surfaces. Transfer to the refrigerator and chill for at least 4 hours until set.

3 Take the mousse out of the refrigerator, dust with cocoa powder, and serve.

TRADITIONAL TIRAMISÙ

SERVES 6

20–24 sponge fingers, about 5½ oz/150 g
2 tbsp cold black coffee
2 tbsp coffee extract
2 tbsp almond liqueur
4 egg yolks
scant ½ cup superfine sugar
a few drops of vanilla extract

grated rind of ½ lemon
heaping 1½ cups mascarpone cheese
2 tsp lemon juice
1 cup heavy cream
1 tbsp milk
¼ cup lightly toasted slivered almonds
2 tbsp unsweetened cocoa
1 tbsp confectioners' sugar

GRANDMA'S TIPS

*This wonderful Italian dessert—
the literal translation is "pick
me up"—is very rich and should
be served in small portions. A
glass of Amaretto is a perfect
accompaniment. This dessert
looks equally as divine when
served in individual ramekins—
divide the ingredients accordingly
for mouthwatering results.*

1 Arrange almost half of the sponge fingers in the bottom of a serving dish. Place the black coffee, coffee extract, and almond liqueur in a bowl and mix. Sprinkle just over half of the mixture over the sponge fingers.

2 Place the egg yolks in a heatproof bowl with the sugar, vanilla extract, and lemon rind. Stand the bowl over a pan of gently simmering water and whisk until very thick and creamy and the whisk leaves a heavy trail when lifted from the bowl.

3 Place the mascarpone cheese in a separate bowl with the lemon juice and beat until smooth. Stir into the egg mixture and, when evenly blended, pour half of the mixture over the sponge fingers and spread out evenly.

4 Add another layer of sponge fingers, sprinkle with the remaining coffee mixture, then cover with the rest of the cheese and egg mixture. Chill in the refrigerator for at least 2 hours, preferably overnight.

5 Whip the cream and milk together until fairly stiff and spread or pipe over the dessert. Sprinkle with the slivered almonds, then sift an even layer of cocoa over the top to cover completely. Finally, sift a layer of confectioners' sugar over the cocoa and serve.

BAKED RICE PUDDING

SERVES 4–6
1 tbsp melted unsalted butter
½ cup white rice
¼ cup superfine sugar
3½ cups whole milk
½ tsp vanilla extract

3 tbsp unsalted butter, chilled and cut
　into pieces
whole nutmeg, for grating
cream, jam, fresh fruit purée, stewed
　fruit, honey, or ice cream, for serving

GRANDMA'S TIPS

In place of nutmeg, you can try grated lemon rind or another spice such as cinnamon to flavor the rice pudding. A handful of raisins or other dried fruit can be added before cooking. If you wish, the rice pudding may be cooked in individual ramekins—just reduce the cooking time to 1–1 ½ hours.

1 Preheat the oven to 300ºF/150ºC. Grease a 4-cup/1.2-liter baking dish (a gratin dish is good) with the melted butter, place the rice in the dish, and sprinkle with the sugar.

2 Heat the milk in a saucepan until almost boiling, then pour over the rice. Add the vanilla extract and stir well to dissolve the sugar.

3 Scatter the bits of butter over the surface of the pudding.

4 Grate the nutmeg over the top, using as much as you like to give it a good covering.

5 Place the dish on a cookie sheet and bake in the center of the oven for 1½–2 hours until the pudding is well browned on top, stirring the pudding after the first half hour of cooking to disperse the rice.

6 Serve hot topped with cream, jam, fresh fruit purée, stewed fruit, honey, or ice cream.

BAKED APPLES

SERVES 4
1 tbsp blanched almonds
⅓ cup dried apricots
1 piece preserved ginger, drained
1 tbsp honey
1 tbsp syrup from the preserved
    ginger jar
4 tbsp rolled oats
4 large baking apples

1 Preheat the oven to 350°F/180°C. Using a sharp knife, chop the almonds very finely. Chop the apricots and preserved ginger very finely. Set aside.

2 Put the honey and syrup in a pan and heat until the honey has melted. Stir in the oats and cook gently over low heat for 2 minutes. Remove the pan from the heat and stir in the almonds, apricots, and preserved ginger.

3 Core the apples, widen the tops slightly and score around the circumference of each to prevent the skins from bursting during cooking. Place them in an ovenproof dish and fill the cavities with the filling. Pour just enough water into the dish to come about one-third of the way up the apples. Bake in the oven for 40 minutes, or until tender. Serve immediately.

BLUEBERRY PANCAKES

MAKES 10–12
1 cup all-purpose flour
2 tbsp superfine sugar
2 tbsp baking powder
½ tsp salt
scant 1 cup buttermilk
3 tbsp unsalted butter, melted

1 large egg
5 oz/140 g fresh blueberries, plus
  extra for serving
sunflower or corn oil, for oiling
butter and warmed maple syrup,
  for serving

GRANDMA'S TIPS

*These small pancakes are ideal
to serve for breakfast with crispy
bacon or scrambled eggs and any
other accompaniment of your
choice.*

1 Preheat the oven to 275°F/140°C. Sift the flour, sugar, baking powder, and salt together into a large bowl and make a well in the center.

2 Beat the buttermilk, butter, and egg together in a separate small bowl, then pour the mixture into the well in the dry ingredients. Beat the dry ingredients into the liquid, gradually drawing them in from the side, until a smooth batter is formed. Gently stir in the blueberries.

3 Heat a large skillet over medium-high heat until a splash of water dances on the surface. Using a pastry brush or crumpled piece of paper towel, oil the base of the skillet.

4 Drop about 4 tablespoons of batter separately into the skillet and spread each out into a 4-inch/10-cm circle. Continue adding as many pancakes as will fit in your skillet. Cook until small bubbles appear on the surface, then flip over with a spatula and cook the pancakes on the other side for an additional 1–2 minutes, or until the bases are golden brown.

5 Transfer the pancakes to a warmed plate and keep warm in the preheated oven while you cook the remaining batter, lightly oiling the skillet as before. Make a stack of the pancakes with parchment paper in between each pancake.

6 Serve with a knob of butter on top of each pancake, extra blueberries on the side, and warm maple syrup for pouring over.

BANANA SPLITS

SERVES 4
4 bananas
6 tbsp chopped mixed nuts, for serving

for the vanilla ice cream
1 1/4 cups milk
1 tsp vanilla extract
3 egg yolks
1/2 cup superfine sugar
1 1/4 cups heavy cream, whipped

for the chocolate rum sauce
4 1/2 oz/125 g semisweet chocolate,
   broken into small pieces
2 1/2 tbsp butter
6 tbsp water
1 tbsp rum

GRANDMA'S TIPS

For a quick and easy dessert, use store-bought ice cream. If you're serving the banana splits to children, omit the rum from the chocolate sauce.

1 To make the ice cream, heat the milk and vanilla extract in a pan until almost boiling. In a bowl, beat together the egg yolks and sugar. Remove the milk from the heat and stir a little into the egg mixture. Transfer the mixture to the pan. Stir over low heat until thick. Do not boil. Remove from the heat. Cool for 30 minutes, fold in the cream, cover with plastic wrap, and chill for 1 hour. Transfer into an ice-cream maker and process for 15 minutes. Alternatively, transfer into a freezerproof container and freeze for 1 hour, then place in a bowl and beat to break up the ice crystals. Put back in the container and freeze for 30 minutes. Repeat twice more, freezing for 30 minutes and whisking each time.

2 To make the sauce, melt the chocolate and butter with the water in a pan, stirring. Remove from the heat and stir in the rum. Peel the bananas, slice them lengthwise, and arrange on 4 serving dishes. Top with ice cream and nuts and serve with the sauce.

Remember the smells of home-baked cakes and cookies when you were young? It was on those days that you learned to rub fat into flour with your fingertips to make pie crusts and to beat sugar and butter together to make cakes. It was fun to sprinkle flour over the kitchen table, roll out cookie dough, and cut it into different shapes—Grandma didn't seem to mind the mess. The best part was eating the misshapen pieces when they were still hot from the oven. This chapter provides recipes for all kinds of delicious goodies—from

GRANDMA'S BAKING DAY

a classic lemon drizzle cake to indulgent chocolate chip brownies. Perhaps it will even encourage you to bake with your own children or grandchildren—they will particularly enjoy helping to make the easy nutty granola bars or assembling the lemon butterfly cupcakes. All of the recipes in this section are perfect for filling those little gaps in the day, be it mid-morning or mid-afternoon—but make sure you put the rest away in an airtight tin so that there will be something delicious on hand when friends or family come by.

CHOCOLATE CAKE

SERVES 8–10
for the cakes
½ cup soft margarine, plus extra
    for greasing
½ cup superfine sugar
2 eggs
1 tbsp light corn syrup
1 cup self-rising flour, sifted
2 tbsp unsweetened cocoa, sifted

for the filling and topping
¼ cup confectioners' sugar, sifted
2 tbsp butter
3½ oz/100 g milk chocolate
a little white chocolate, melted (optional)

GRANDMA'S TIPS

A simple chocolate layer cake is a good base for all sorts of cakes. It is ideal as a birthday cake to decorate as you wish, or to serve with raspberries and cream for a summer dessert.

1 Preheat the oven to 325°F/160°C. Lightly grease two 7-inch/18-cm shallow cake pans.

2 Place all of the ingredients for the cake in a large mixing bowl and beat with a wooden spoon or electric hand whisk to form a smooth mixture.

3 Divide the mixture between the prepared pans and level the tops. Bake in the preheated oven for 20 minutes, or until springy to the touch. Cool for a few minutes in the pans before transferring to a wire rack to cool completely.

4 To make the filling, beat the confectioners' sugar and butter together in a bowl until light and fluffy. Melt the milk chocolate and beat half into the filling mixture. Use the filling to sandwich the 2 cakes together.

5 Spread the remaining melted milk chocolate over the top of the cake. Pipe circles of contrasting melted white chocolate and then feather them into the milk chocolate with a toothpick, if desired. Let the topping set before serving.

SPONGE LAYER CAKE

SERVES 8–10

¾ cup unsalted butter, at room
   temperature, plus extra for greasing
¾ cup superfine sugar
3 eggs, beaten

scant 1½ cups self-rising flour
pinch of salt
3 tbsp raspberry jam
1 tbsp superfine or confectioners' sugar

GRANDMA'S TIPS

This cake can also be flavored with grated lemon rind and sandwiched together with lemon curd to give it a summery feel. For a simple buttercream filling, whisk together equal quantities of butter and confectioners' sugar until light and fluffy.

1 Preheat the oven to 350°F/180°C.

2 Grease two 8-inch/20-cm round cake pans and line with wax or parchment paper.

3 Cream the butter and superfine sugar together in a mixing bowl using a wooden spoon or a handheld mixer until the mixture is pale in color and light and fluffy.

4 Add the eggs, one at a time, beating well after each addition.

5 Sift the flour and salt together into a separate bowl and carefully add to the mixture, folding it in with a metal spoon or a spatula.

6 Divide the mixture between the pans and smooth over with a spatula.

7 Place the pans in the center of the oven and bake for 25–30 minutes until well risen, golden brown, and beginning to shrink from the sides of the pan.

8 Remove from the oven and let stand for 1 minute.

9 Loosen the cakes from around the edge of the pans using a palette knife. Turn the cakes out onto a clean kitchen towel, remove the paper, and invert the cakes onto a wire rack (this prevents the wire rack from marking the top of the cakes).

10 When completely cool, sandwich together the cakes with the jam and sprinkle with the superfine or confectioners' sugar. The cake is delicious when freshly baked, but any remaining cake can be stored in an airtight container for up to 1 week.

LEMON DRIZZLE CAKE

SERVES 8
butter, for greasing
1¾ cups all-purpose flour
2 tsp baking powder
1 cup superfine sugar
4 eggs
⅔ cup sour cream
grated rind of 1 large lemon
4 tbsp lemon juice
⅔ cup sunflower oil

for the syrup
4 tbsp confectioners' sugar
3 tbsp lemon juice

1 Preheat the oven to 350°F/180°C. Lightly grease an 8-inch/20-cm loose-bottom round cake pan and line the base with parchment paper.

2 Sift the flour and baking powder into a mixing bowl and stir in the superfine sugar.

3 In a separate bowl, whisk the eggs, sour cream, lemon rind, lemon juice, and oil together.

4 Pour the egg mixture into the dry ingredients and mix well until evenly combined.

5 Pour the mixture into the prepared pan and bake in the preheated oven for 45–60 minutes, or until risen and golden brown.

6 Meanwhile, to make the syrup, mix together the confectioners' sugar and lemon juice in a small pan. Stir over low heat until just beginning to bubble and turn syrupy.

7 As soon as the cake comes out of the oven, prick the surface with a fine skewer, then brush the syrup over the top. Let the cake cool completely in the pan before turning out and serving.

RICH FRUIT CAKE

SERVES 12
butter, for greasing
1 cup pitted unsweetened dates
¾ cup dried prunes
scant 1 cup unsweetened orange juice
2 tbsp molasses
1 tsp finely grated lemon rind
1 tsp finely grated orange rind
1½ cups whole wheat self-rising flour
1 tsp ground allspice
¾ cup seedless raisins

¾ cup golden raisins
¾ cup currants
¾ cup dried cranberries
3 large eggs, separated

for decorating
1 tbsp apricot jelly, warmed
confectioners' sugar, for dusting
6 oz/175 g sugar paste
strips of orange rind
strips of lemon rind

GRANDMA'S TIPS

*This healthy take on the
typically rich fruit cake makes
an ideal Christmas or celebration
cake. It keeps well in an airtight
tin and can be covered with
marzipan and royal icing and
decorated with Christmas figures
or flowers.*

1 Grease and line a deep 8-inch/20-cm round cake pan. Chop the dates and prunes and place in a large, heavy-bottom pan. Pour over the orange juice and let simmer for 10 minutes. Remove the pan from the heat and beat the fruit mixture until puréed. Add the molasses and citrus rinds and let cool.

2 Preheat the oven to 325°F/160°C. Sift the flour and allspice into a bowl, adding any bran that remains in the strainer. Add the raisins, golden raisins, currants, and dried cranberries. When the date and prune mixture is cool, whisk in the egg yolks. Whisk the egg whites in a clean bowl until stiff. Spoon the fruit mixture into the dry ingredients and mix together. Gently fold in the egg whites. Transfer to the prepared pan and bake in the preheated oven for 1½ hours. Let cool in the pan.

3 Remove the cake from the pan and brush the top with jelly. Dust the counter with confectioners' sugar and roll out the sugar paste thinly. Lay the sugar paste over the top of the cake and trim the edges. Decorate with orange and lemon rind.

CLASSIC CARROT CAKE

SERVES 12
butter, for greasing
1 cup self-rising flour
pinch of salt
1 tsp ground cinnamon
¾ cup light brown sugar
2 eggs
scant ½ cup sunflower oil
4½ oz/125 g carrot, peeled and
   finely grated
⅓ cup shredded coconut
⅓ cup walnuts, chopped
walnut pieces, for decorating

for the frosting
4 tbsp butter, softened
1¾ oz soft cheese
1½ cups confectioners' sugar, sifted
1 tsp lemon juice

GRANDMA'S TIPS

This cake freezes well (before frosting) and can be kept for up to three months. It's perfect for an afternoon treat as well as a quick dessert served with ice cream.

1 Preheat the oven to 350°F/180°C. Lightly grease an 8-inch/20-cm square cake pan and line the base with parchment paper.

2 Sift the flour, salt, and ground cinnamon into a large bowl and stir in the brown sugar. Add the eggs and oil to the dry ingredients and mix well.

3 Stir in the grated carrot, shredded coconut, and chopped walnuts.

4 Pour the mixture into the prepared pan and bake in the preheated oven for 20–25 minutes, or until just firm to the touch. Let cool in the pan.

5 Meanwhile, make the frosting. In a bowl, beat together the butter, soft cheese, confectioners' sugar, and lemon juice, until the mixture is fluffy and creamy.

6 Turn the cake out of the pan and cut into 12 bars or slices. Spread with the frosting and then decorate with walnut pieces.

APPLE STREUSEL CAKE

SERVES 8
½ cup butter, plus extra for greasing
1 lb/450 g baking apples
1¼ cups self-rising flour
1 tsp ground cinnamon
pinch of salt
heaping ½ cup superfine sugar
2 eggs

1–2 tbsp milk
confectioners' sugar, for dusting

for the streusel topping
heaping ¾ cup self-rising flour
6 tbsp butter
scant ½ cup superfine sugar

1 Preheat the oven to 350°F/180°C, then grease a 9-inch/23-cm springform cake pan. To make the streusel topping, sift the flour into a bowl and rub in the butter until the mixture resembles coarse crumbs. Stir in the sugar and set aside.

2 Peel, core, and thinly slice the apples. To make the cake, sift the flour into a bowl with the cinnamon and salt. Place the butter and sugar in a separate bowl and beat together until light and fluffy. Gradually beat in the eggs, adding a little of the flour mixture with the last addition of egg. Gently fold in half the remaining flour mixture, then fold in the rest with the milk.

3 Spoon the batter into the prepared pan and smooth the top. Cover with the sliced apples and sprinkle the streusel topping evenly over the top. Bake in the preheated oven for 1 hour, or until browned and firm to the touch. Let cool in the pan before opening the sides. Dust the cake with confectioners' sugar before serving.

COFFEE &
WALNUT CAKE

SERVES 8
for the frosting
6 tbsp unsweetened cocoa
2 tbsp cornstarch
6 tbsp superfine sugar
½ cup strong black coffee, cooled
1 cup milk

for the sponge
2 cups all-purpose flour
1 tbsp baking powder
7½ tbsp superfine sugar
6 tbsp butter, softened, plus extra
    for greasing
2 eggs
⅔ cup milk
3 tbsp hot strong black coffee
½ cup chopped walnuts
½ cup golden raisins
walnut halves, for decorating

GRANDMA'S TIPS
This soft-textured cake is always very popular. The chocolate topping can be replaced with a simple sugar icing if you prefer.

1 To make the frosting, put all the ingredients into a food processor and process until creamy. Transfer to a pan and heat, stirring, over medium heat until bubbling. Cook for 1 minute, then pour into a heatproof bowl. Let cool, then cover with plastic wrap and refrigerate for at least 2 hours.

2 Preheat the oven to 375°F/190°C. Grease a 9-inch/23-cm loose-bottomed cake pan with butter and line with parchment paper.

3 To make the sponge, sift the flour and baking powder into a bowl, then stir in the sugar. In a separate bowl, beat together the butter, eggs, milk, and coffee, then mix into the flour mixture. Stir in the chopped walnuts and the golden raisins. Spoon the batter into the prepared cake pan and level the surface. Transfer to the preheated oven and bake for 1 hour. Remove from the oven and let cool. When cool enough to handle, turn out on to a wire rack and let cool completely. Spread the frosting over the top of the cooled cake, decorate with the walnut halves, and serve.

GINGERBREAD

MAKES 12–16
3¾ cups all-purpose flour
1 tbsp baking powder
1 tsp baking soda
1 tbsp ground ginger
¾ cup unsalted butter
¾ cup brown sugar

¾ cup blackstrap molasses
¾ cup maple syrup or corn syrup
1 egg, beaten
1 cup milk
cream or warmed maple syrup,
   for serving

1 Line a 9-inch/23-cm square cake pan, 2 inches/5 cm deep, with wax or parchment paper.

2 Preheat the oven to 325°F/160°C.

3 Sift the flour, baking powder, baking soda, and ground ginger into a large mixing bowl.

4 Place the butter, brown sugar, molasses, and maple syrup in a medium saucepan and heat over low heat until the butter has melted and the sugar has dissolved. Set aside to cool briefly.

5 Mix the beaten egg with the milk and add to the cooled syrup mixture.

6 Add the liquid ingredients to the dry ingredients and beat well using a wooden spoon until the mixture is smooth and glossy.

7 Pour the mixture into the prepared pan and bake in the center of the oven for 1½ hours until well risen and just firm to the touch. This makes a lovely sticky gingerbread, but if you like a firmer cake cook for an additional 15 minutes.

8 Remove from the oven and allow the cake to cool in the pan on a wire rack. When cooled, remove the cake from the pan with the wax paper. To store, wrap with foil and place in an airtight container for up to 1 week to allow the flavors to develop.

9 Cut into wedges and serve as an afternoon snack or with cream for dessert. Drizzling some warmed maple syrup on top is an added extravagance.

MARBLED CHOCOLATE &
ORANGE CAKE

SERVES 12

⅔ cup butter, softened, plus extra for greasing
2¾ oz/75 g semisweet chocolate, broken into pieces
1¼ cups superfine sugar

5 large eggs, beaten
heaping 1 cup all-purpose flour
2 tsp baking powder
pinch of salt
grated rind of 2 oranges

1 Preheat the oven to 350°F/180°C. Grease and line the bottom and ends of two 1-lb/450-g loaf pans. Place the chocolate in a heatproof bowl set over a pan of simmering water, making sure that the bottom of the bowl does not touch the water. Remove from the heat once the chocolate has melted.

2 Place the butter and sugar in a separate bowl and beat until light and fluffy. Gradually beat in the eggs. Sift the flour, baking powder, and salt into the mixture and fold in.

3 Transfer one-third of the mixture to the melted chocolate and stir. Stir the orange rind into the remaining mixture and spread one-quarter of the mixture evenly in each cake pan.

4 Drop spoonfuls of the chocolate mixture on top, dividing it between the 2 pans, but do not smooth it out. Divide the remaining orange mixture between the 2 pans, then, using a knife, gently swirl the top 2 layers together to give a marbled effect. Bake in the preheated oven for 35–40 minutes, or until a skewer inserted into the center comes out clean.

5 Let cool in the pans for 10 minutes, then turn out, peel off the lining paper, and transfer to a wire rack to cool completely.

BANANA LOAF

SERVES 6
unsalted butter, for greasing
scant 1 cup white self-rising flour
scant ¾ cup light brown self-rising flour
heaping ¾ cup raw brown sugar
pinch of salt
½ tsp ground cinnamon
½ tsp ground nutmeg
2 large ripe bananas, peeled
¾ cup orange juice
2 eggs, beaten
4 tbsp canola oil
honey, for serving

GRANDMA'S TIPS

This loaf is delicious simply buttered or served with chopped banana, walnuts, and a drizzling of honey. Try toasting a slice or two the next day to bring out the banana flavor even more.

1 Preheat the oven to 350°F/180°C. Lightly grease and line a 1-lb/450-g loaf pan.

2 Sift the flours, sugar, a pinch of salt, and the spices into a large bowl.

3 In a separate bowl, mash the bananas with the orange juice, then stir in the eggs and oil. Pour into the dry ingredients and mix well.

4 Spoon into the prepared loaf pan and bake in the preheated oven for 1 hour, then test to see if it is cooked by inserting a skewer into the center. If it comes out clean, the loaf is done. If not, bake for an additional 10 minutes and test again.

5 Remove from the oven and let cool in the pan. Turn the loaf out, slice, and serve with honey.

STRAWBERRY ROULADE

SERVES 8
3 large eggs
⅔ cup superfine sugar
scant 1 cup all-purpose flour
1 tbsp hot water

for the filling
¾ cup lowfat mascarpone cheese
1 tsp almond extract
1 cup small strawberries
1 tbsp slivered almonds, toasted
confectioners' sugar, for dusting

GRANDMA'S TIPS

Making a roulade looks quite difficult, but it really is quite simple when you use parchment paper. Try varying the filling by using raspberries instead of the strawberries or whipped cream instead of the mascarpone. For a simpler roulade, fill with fruit conserve—this makes a good base for a trifle.

1 Preheat the oven to 425°F/220°C. Line a 14 x 10-inch/35 x 25-cm jelly roll pan with parchment paper. Place the eggs in a large, heatproof bowl with the superfine sugar, place over a pan of hot water and, using an electric beater, beat until pale and thick.

2 Remove the bowl from the pan. Sift in the flour and fold into the eggs with the hot water. Pour the mixture into the prepared pan and bake in the preheated oven for 8–10 minutes, or until golden and set.

3 Transfer the sponge to a sheet of parchment paper. Carefully peel off the lining paper and roll up the sponge tightly, along with the parchment paper. Wrap the sponge in a dish towel and let cool until completely cooled.

4 Mix the mascarpone cheese and almond extract together in a bowl. Let the mixture chill in the refrigerator until ready to use. Set aside a few strawberries for the decoration, wash, hull, and slice the rest.

5 Unroll the sponge, spread the mascarpone cheese mixture over the sponge and sprinkle with the sliced strawberries. Roll the sponge up again and transfer to a serving plate. Sprinkle with almonds and lightly dust with confectioners' sugar. Decorate with the reserved strawberries and serve.

CHOCOLATE CHIP
BROWNIES

MAKES 12

1 cup butter, softened, plus extra
   for greasing
5½ oz/150 g semisweet chocolate,
   broken into pieces
heaping 1½ cups self-rising flour

scant ⅔ cup superfine sugar
4 eggs, beaten
⅔ cup shelled pistachios, chopped
3½ oz/100 g white chocolate,
   coarsely chopped
confectioners' sugar, for dusting

1 Preheat the oven to 350°F/180°C. Grease a 9-inch/23-cm square baking pan and line
with parchment paper.

2 Place the chocolate and softened butter in a heatproof bowl set over a pan of
simmering water. Stir until melted, then let cool slightly.

3 Sift the flour into a separate bowl and stir in the superfine sugar.

4 Stir the beaten eggs into the chocolate mixture, then pour the mixture into the flour
and sugar and beat well. Stir in the pistachios and white chocolate, then pour the mixture
into the pan, using a spatula to spread it evenly.

5 Bake in the preheated oven for 30–35 minutes, or until firm to the touch around
the edges. Let cool in the pan for 20 minutes. Turn out onto a wire rack. Dust with
confectioners' sugar and let cool completely. Cut into 12 pieces and serve.

NUTTY GRANOLA BARS

MAKES 16

½ cup butter, plus extra for greasing
scant 2¾ cups rolled oats
¾ cup chopped hazelnuts

6 tbsp all-purpose flour
2 tbsp corn syrup
scant ½ cup brown sugar

GRANDMA'S TIPS

These bars are very handy for lunch boxes or to bring along on a picnic. Honey can be used instead of corn syrup and dried fruit, such as apricots or cranberries, can be added for color and flavor.

1 Preheat the oven to 350°F/180°C, then grease a 9-inch/23-cm square ovenproof dish or cake pan. Place the rolled oats, chopped hazelnuts, and flour in a large mixing bowl and stir together.

2 Place the butter, corn syrup, and sugar in a pan over low heat and stir until melted. Pour onto the dry ingredients and mix well. Turn into the prepared ovenproof dish and smooth the surface with the back of a spoon.

3 Bake in the oven for 20–25 minutes, or until golden and firm to the touch. Mark into 16 pieces and let cool in the dish. When completely cooled, cut through with a sharp knife and remove from the dish.

LEMON BUTTERFLY
CUPCAKES

MAKES 12
generous ¾ cup self-rising flour
½ tsp baking powder
½ cup butter, softened
heaping ½ cup superfine sugar
2 eggs, beaten
finely grated rind of ½ lemon

2–4 tbsp milk
confectioners' sugar, for dusting

for the filling
¼ cup butter
heaping 1 cup confectioners' sugar
1 tbsp lemon juice

GRANDMA'S TIPS

Cupcakes are always a favorite for children's parties. You can use multicolored paper cases to make them even more attractive. A whole strawberry, raspberry, or candied cherry can be popped on top to decorate.

1 Preheat the oven to 375°F/190°C. Place 12 paper cases in a muffin pan. Sift the flour and baking powder into a bowl. Add the butter, sugar, eggs, lemon rind, and enough milk to give a medium-soft consistency. Beat thoroughly until smooth. Divide the batter among the paper cases and bake in the preheated oven for 15–20 minutes, or until well risen and golden. Transfer to wire racks to cool.

2 To make the filling, place the butter in a bowl, then sift in the confectioners' sugar and add the lemon juice. Beat well until smooth and creamy. When the cakes are completely cooled, use a sharp-pointed vegetable knife to cut a circle from the top of each cake, then cut each circle in half.

3 Spoon a little of the buttercream into the center of each cake and press the 2 semi-circular pieces into it to resemble wings. Dust the cakes with sifted confectioners' sugar before serving.

BLUEBERRY MUFFINS

MAKES 10–12

1⅔ cups all-purpose flour
1 tsp baking powder
pinch of salt
½ cup raw brown sugar, plus
    1 tbsp for sprinkling

1 egg, beaten
scant 1 cup milk
4 tbsp unsalted butter, melted
4½ oz/125 g small fresh blueberries

1 Preheat the oven to 350°F/180°C. Line a 12-hole muffin pan with paper cases. Sift the flour, baking powder, and salt into a large bowl and stir in the sugar.

2 Add the beaten egg, milk, and melted butter to the dry ingredients and stir in lightly until just combined—do not overmix. Carefully fold in the blueberries.

3 Spoon the mixture into the paper cases, taking care not to overfill, and sprinkle with the remaining sugar.

4 Bake in the preheated oven for 25–30 minutes, or until golden brown and firm. Transfer to a wire rack to cool a little.

BISCUITS

MAKES 10–12
3½ cups all-purpose flour, plus extra
    for dusting
½ tsp salt
2 tsp baking powder
4 tbsp butter

2 tbsp superfine sugar
1 cup milk
3 tbsp milk, for glazing
strawberry conserves and whipped heavy
    cream, for serving

GRANDMA'S TIPS

*These delicious biscuits are at
their best straight from the oven.
You can also add 2 oz/55 g
dried mixed fruit to the dough if
you like. For savory biscuits to
serve with soup, add 2 oz/55 g
grated cheese to the mix and
omit the sugar.*

1 Preheat the oven to 425°F/220°C.

2 Sift the flour, salt, and baking powder into a bowl. Rub in the butter until the mixture resembles breadcrumbs. Stir in the sugar.

3 Make a well in the center and pour in the milk. Stir in using a palette knife and make a soft dough.

4 Turn the mixture onto a floured surface and lightly flatten the dough until it is of an even thickness, about ½ inch/1 cm. Don't be heavy-handed, biscuits need a light touch.

5 Use a 2½-inch/6-cm cookie cutter to cut out the biscuits and place on the baking sheet.

6 Glaze with a little milk and bake for 10–12 minutes, until golden and well risen.

7 Cool on a wire rack and serve freshly baked with strawberry conserves and whipped heavy cream.

SHORTBREAD

MAKES 8

½ cup butter, cut into small pieces, plus
    extra for greasing
scant 1½ cups all-purpose flour, plus
    extra for dusting

pinch of salt
4 tbsp superfine sugar, plus extra
    for dusting

GRANDMA'S TIPS

*To give the shortbread a bit more
texture, replace 2 oz/55 g of
the flour with semolina, which
will give it a more granular,
slightly gritty texture.*

1 Preheat the oven to 300°F/150°C.

2 Grease an 8-inch/20-cm fluted tart pan.

3 Mix together the flour, salt, and sugar. Rub the butter into the dry ingredients. Continue to work the mixture until it forms a soft dough. Make sure you do not overwork the shortbread or it will be tough, not crumbly as it should be.

4 Lightly press the dough into the tart pan. If you don't have a fluted pan, roll out the dough on a lightly floured board, place on a baking sheet and pinch the edges to form a scalloped pattern.

5 Mark into 8 pieces with a knife. Prick all over with a fork and bake in the center of the oven for 45–50 minutes until the shortbread is firm and just colored.

6 Allow to cool in the tin and dust with the sugar. Cut into portions and remove to a wire rack. Store in an airtight container in a cool place until needed.

CHOCOLATE CHIP
COOKIES

MAKES 18
1½ cups all-purpose flour, sifted
1 tsp baking powder
½ cup soft margarine, plus extra
   for greasing

scant ⅔ cup light brown sugar
¼ cup superfine sugar
½ tsp vanilla extract
1 egg
⅔ cup semisweet chocolate chips

1 Preheat the oven to 375°F/190°C. Place all the ingredients in a large mixing bowl and beat until they are thoroughly combined.

2 Lightly grease 2 cookie sheets. Place tablespoonfuls of the mixture onto the cookie sheets, spacing them well apart to allow for spreading during cooking.

3 Bake in the oven for 10–12 minutes until the cookies are golden brown.

4 Using a spatula, transfer the cookies to a cooling rack to cool completely before serving.

GINGERSNAPS

MAKES 30
½ cup butter, plus extra for greasing
3 cups self-rising flour
pinch of salt
1 cup superfine sugar

1 tbsp ground ginger
1 tsp baking soda
¼ cup light corn syrup
1 egg, beaten
1 tsp grated orange rind

GRANDMA'S TIPS
You may find it easier to roll out the dough into a log shape and then cut into slices before placing the gingersnaps on the cookie sheets.

1 Preheat the oven to 325°F/160°C. Lightly grease several cookie sheets.

2 Sift the flour, salt, sugar, ginger, and baking soda into a mixing bowl.

3 Heat the butter and light corn syrup in a pan over very low heat until the butter has melted.

4 Let the butter mixture cool slightly, then pour it onto the dry ingredients.

5 Add the egg and orange rind and mix thoroughly.

6 Using your hands, carefully shape the dough into 30 even-size balls.

7 Place the balls well apart on the prepared cookie sheets, then flatten them slightly with your fingers.

8 Bake in the preheated oven for 15–20 minutes, then transfer the cookies to a wire rack to cool.

CLASSIC OATMEAL
COOKIES

MAKES 30
¾ cup butter or margarine, plus extra
   for greasing
scant 1⅓ cups raw brown sugar
1 egg
4 tbsp water

1 tsp vanilla extract
4⅓ cups rolled oats
1 cup all-purpose flour
1 tsp salt
½ tsp baking soda

GRANDMA'S TIPS

After you've made these classic cookies once, why not vary them by substituting desiccated coconut for some of the oats? You could also add some chopped nuts, chopped candied cherries, or chocolate chips.

1 Preheat the oven to 350°F/180°C and grease a large cookie sheet.

2 Cream the butter and sugar together in a large mixing bowl. Beat in the egg, water, and vanilla extract until the mixture is smooth.

3 In a separate bowl, mix the oats, flour, salt, and baking soda. Gradually stir the oat mixture into the butter mixture until thoroughly combined.

4 Put 30 rounded tablespoonfuls of cookie mixture onto the greased cookie sheet, making sure they are well spaced. Transfer to the preheated oven and bake for 15 minutes, or until the cookies are golden brown.

5 Remove the cookies from the oven and place on a wire rack to cool before serving.

WHITE BREAD

MAKES 1 LARGE LOAF

4 cups white bread flour, plus 2 tbsp for
  dusting
1 tsp salt

¼ oz/7 g active dry yeast
1 tbsp vegetable oil or melted butter,
  plus 1 tsp for greasing
1¼ cups lukewarm water

1 Mix the flour, salt, and yeast together in a mixing bowl. Add the oil and water and stir well to form a soft dough.

2 Turn the dough out onto a lightly floured board and knead well by hand for 5–7 minutes. Alternatively, use a freestanding electric mixer for this and knead the dough with the dough hook for 4–5 minutes. The dough should have a smooth appearance and feel elastic.

3 Return the dough to the bowl, cover with plastic wrap, and let rise in a warm place for 1 hour. When it has doubled in size, turn it out onto a floured board and knead again for 30 seconds; this is known as "punching down." Knead it until smooth.

4 Shape the dough into a rectangle the length of the pan and three times the width. Grease the pan well, fold the dough into three lengthwise, and put it in the pan with the seam underneath for a well-shaped loaf. Cover and let rise in a warm place for 30 minutes until it has risen well above the pan.

5 Preheat the oven to 425°F/220°C. Bake in the center of the preheated oven for 25–30 minutes until firm and golden brown. Test that the loaf is cooked by tapping it on the base—it should sound hollow. Cool on a cooling rack for 30 minutes. Store in an airtight container in a cool place for 3–4 days.

Index